CW00839919

The Science of Self-Discipline:

The Willpower, Mental Toughness, and Self-Control to Resist Temptation and Achieve Your Goals

By Peter Hollins,
Author and Researcher at
petehollins.com

Table of Contents

Introduction

When I was younger, I was bullied about my weight.

This might sound like a familiar story, but mine is a little bit different because I was constantly picked on for being skinny as a pole. Once when we had a large windstorm, I literally left my feet because of the wind.

Beanpole, feather, stickman, skeletor, the skeleton, boneboy. These were just some of the nicknames that were hurled my way, and luckily, none of them stuck for more than a few days. I thought when I went to university, the teasing would stop because we weren't children anymore; we were real adults living on our own and running our own lives. Now, there are a few fallacious parts of that statement, but most relevant to this story, the teasing only intensified. I had severely underestimated the ego of the male aged 18–22 years.

So I spent my first year of university hearing many of the same nicknames I had heard when I was younger. They really hadn't evolved much since. When I moved into the dorms my second year of university, I was lucky enough to be randomly assigned a former football player as my roommate. This roommate, Mike, went on to become a fairly successful personal trainer, which is relevant to the story because I believe I was his first guinea pig. I told him I wanted to gain weight and stop being teased, and he made it his goal that year to make my wish a reality.

We discovered that I simply didn't eat enough, even when I thought I had gorged myself three times in one day. We tracked calories rigorously and found that I needed, on average, an extra 1,000 calories a day to gain weight at a rapid but healthy pace. If you're wondering where self-discipline comes into the story, it's right here. Unlike many people struggling with weight, I had to discipline myself to eat on schedule five times a day. Yes, for some of you, this sounds like a fantasy. But for anyone skinny trying to gain weight, it is just as much a nightmare as only being able to eat one meal a day. It's veritable torture trying to stuff yourself multiple times a day, only to have to do the same thing the next day and the next.

I probably would have given up after the first week if it weren't for Mike. Luckily for me, we were in most of the same classes, and he was my constant companion in reminding me to eat, asking me how much I had eaten that day, and even taking me to get ice cream when I still needed calories. I didn't know it at the time, but I had created an environment for myself that forced self-discipline. Whenever I didn't have it myself, I had Mike to push me and remind me exactly what I was working so hard for.

Two months later, I had gained 11 pounds. The journey continued for years, but this was my first introduction to the intentional exercise of self-discipline. I saw where it could get me, and I now see that it's a necessary trait in everything we do. For whatever goal you want to achieve, there is discomfort along that path. Self-discipline drives you through this discomfort and allows you to achieve and attain. It's an essential component of mastery, and nothing great was ever accomplished without it.

But it doesn't live within a vacuum. Oftentimes, we have the best of intentions, only to be distracted by an errant shiny object or dog. Just grinding your teeth and pushing isn't always enough. In this book, I discuss and teach how to increase your baseline level of self-discipline, as well as how to engineer your life as to not need self-discipline at every twist and turn.

You might get lucky just like me and already live in close proximity to someone that enforces your sense of discipline whether you like it or not. But if you don't, there are countless ways to decisively take control of your life and to no longer fall prey to your wayward impulses and distractions. Self-discipline is not only the goal, but also the journey.

Chapter 1. The Biological Basis of Self-Discipline

Noted author and speaker Jim Rohn once said, "We must all suffer one of two things: the pain of discipline or the pain of regret." Throughout your life, you can make a choice as to how you suffer; discipline is usually what keeps you from what you truly want.

Having self-discipline and willpower is the ability to do difficult or unpleasant things because those things are better for your well-being in the long run. That could mean waking up early to exercise when you would rather press the snooze button, or maybe resisting the temptation of a sugary snack that you know will result in an energy crash an hour later. Whatever you need to do in order to accomplish your goals and to be fulfilled, discipline will be a crucial skill in that process. On the other side of the spectrum, a life devoid of discipline is necessarily one filled with regret because nothing worth doing will ever come to fruition.

The focus of this book is to ingrain self-discipline and willpower as an unconscious habit to ensure that you can consistently achieve your goals and live without regret. Waking up five minutes earlier in the morning may not mean much on a daily basis, but there is a hugely cumulative effect that leads you to the path of success. Just like the athlete warms up and stretches her muscles before a race, self-discipline is a quality to be honed.

The Biological Basis of Self-Discipline

First, it is important to understand how self-discipline manifests biologically. Without understanding what causes, diminishes, or strengthens it from a neurological perspective, we are unable to act to benefit it. It would be like trying to treat a sickness without understanding what caused it. Pinpointing the physical origins of complex behaviors in the brain is a difficult and ongoing process for neuroscientists and psychologists. You won't find the words "impulsivity" and "willpower" etched into specific places in our brains, nor is there an easy chemical hack for sustainably altering those functions.

It's estimated that the average human brain has some 100 billion neurons—the tiny cells that travel through our brain circuitry to produce our thoughts and behaviors. That's about the same number as there are stars in the Milky Way Galaxy, and so it's no wonder that scientists have only just begun to understand the connections between neurons and the outcomes they generate. Recent experiments have begun providing some clues about the inner workings of our minds.

Todd Hare and Colin Camerer in 2009 used functional magnetic resonance imaging machines, or fMRIs, in order to examine the brain activity that takes place when people are performing certain tasks requiring elements of discipline and self-control. Through this, they were able to see increased activity in a region of the brain called the *ventral medial prefrontal cortex* while the study's participants were deciding between accepting a large monetary reward in the future or a smaller reward immediately—the classic struggle of delayed gratification and willpower.

The *dorsolateral prefrontal cortex*—another region of the brain's decision-making hub—was also shown to play a role when we are weighing our future and immediate options. There was a correlation between higher activity in this region and choosing options that had better long-term consequences—the larger but delayed monetary reward, or the healthier food item, for example.

These fMRI studies demonstrate that the ability to make healthier long-term decisions and engage in self-discipline comes more easily to some people than others as a result of the activity and structure of their prefrontal cortex. In other words, they were able to literally identify the areas of the brain responsible for discipline.

Why is this significant? Because of the concept of neuroplasticity—the ability of the brain to constantly form and reorganize synaptic connections—we know that the amount of self-control somebody possesses is anything but static. The phrase "exercise your self-control" is an accurate way of thinking about your ability to be disciplined in the face of temptation, as that ability can be built up if you consistently exercise it by making healthier choices, and it can also be stripped down by constantly giving in to unhealthy pleasures. If you are the type of person that can never refuse donuts in the cafeteria, who struggles with maintaining a consistent exercise routine, or who simply wishes to quit bad habits or create good ones, this is refreshing news. You can improve and get better and you are not doomed.

A 2011 brain imaging study conducted by a team of 14 researchers re-examined volunteers who had participated as children in the Stanford Marshmallow Experiment—a famous study on delaying gratification that had been conducted some four decades prior and that will be covered in greater detail later.

The researchers found that those who were able to delay gratification in the original Stanford study had more active prefrontal cortices as well as key differences in the ventral striatum—a brain region linked to addictions—in their mid-life when they were trying to exercise self-control while enticed to make unhealthy choices. They were also uniformly more successful by almost all conventional means. These biological differences may have started out small, but were significant in later years.

Given our still limited understanding of the human brain, it's impossible to say how much of your self-discipline comes from a genetic predisposition and how much of it is determined by your environment and upbringing. What we can say confidently is that wherever you began, it is possible to change and improve your self-discipline. Running exercises the legs; therefore, targeting the legs will improve fitness. It is the same with the brain areas identified in the various studies.

You shouldn't feel discouraged if you struggle with self-control and discipline in your adulthood. It certainly would have been easier to learn those skills when you were younger, just as languages have been proven to be easier to learn when young, but that in no way makes it impossible to do so now. Self-discipline and willpower can be consistently exercised to achieve sustainable improvements over time. As with any skill, the more you practice being disciplined, the better you become at it.

These studies also provide fairly strong evidence against spoiling children. Always getting your way in childhood means that the brain structures that underlie discipline are neglected and underutilized, culminating in an adult that isn't familiar with controlling urges and thinking about long-term consequences. You can imagine how this might play out in daily life.

Focus and Executive Functions

Focus is one of the main pillars of self-discipline; a person who lacks the ability to focus is almost certainly one who will also lack discipline. Focus itself is dependent on something that neuroscientists call *executive functions*.

The three executive functions that we are most concerned with when it comes to being disciplined are working memory, impulse control, and cognitive flexibility and adaptability. You can see why they are aptly named the executive functions. Your brain has to be able to set and pursue goals, prioritize activities, filter distractions, and control unhelpful inhibitions.

Together, these functions have been shown to take place in several brain regions including the dorsolateral prefrontal cortex, the anterior cingulate cortex, and the orbitofrontal cortex, in addition to the supplementary motor area and the cingulate motor zones. Just like with self-discipline and willpower, the association with specific brain structures means you can target and improve them specifically.

It's clearly desirable to have more blood flow to those regions of the brain that are responsible for executive functions in order to improve and refresh discipline. For many years, meditation has been touted as a panacea for all sorts of problems, including a lack of focus and discipline. Somewhat surprisingly to the skeptics out there, studies have confirmed that the practice of meditation does indeed have a real effect. MRI scans were taken of volunteers before and after they participated in an eight-week mindfulness course, the results of which make a strong case for meditation being a useful tool for "strengthening" the areas of the brain that are responsible for executive functions, and thus self-discipline.

Moreover, meditation was shown to shrink the amygdala, which is generally responsible for the primal emotions, instincts, and drives that keep us alive. It is also the center of the "fight-or-flight" instinct, which heightens our arousal (for better or worse) in the face of a perceived threat. It's the body's alarm system. This means participants who meditated would be less susceptible to fear, emotional impulses, and stress. Self-discipline is often sabotaged by emotional impulses and stress, so keeping these under control is helpful to setting the conditions for willpower.

On top of that, the scans showed that the gray matter in the prefrontal cortex had become noticeably denser. The gray matter growth wasn't isolated to just the prefrontal cortex. The brain structure located behind the frontal lobe—the anterior cingulate cortex—also became denser with meditation practice. This brain area has been associated with functions having to do with self-regulation, such as monitoring attention conflicts and allowing for greater cognitive flexibility. In other words, meditation can both reduce the feelings and emotions that make us lose self-control and increase our ability to manage those feelings by physically improving the brain structures responsible for them.

If meditation isn't already a part of your daily routine, consider adding it in. It's common to hear people say that they don't have time for meditation, possibly even seeing this as scheduling a time to be unproductive. But if meditating for a few minutes a day can make you more capable of carrying out executive functions, the increased focus and discipline while you are active will more than make up for a few minutes of inactivity.

It's nearly impossible to achieve focus and self-discipline separately. Being disciplined in your pursuit of long-term goals is only possible if you can consistently focus on the decisions and actions that lead to accomplishing those goals.

Willpower Fatigue

Due to its biological basis, willpower and self-discipline are not static quantities you can maintain in the face of constant temptation. They are more similar to a gas tank. Using your willpower will deplete it, just the same as lifting weights would fatigue your muscles.

Individuals who are experiencing willpower depletion have also been shown to have decreased cognitive activity in the brain as well as lower blood-glucose levels relative to people who haven't had to exercise willpower. The brains of people who resist the cookie once are different from the brain of someone who has had to resist a cookie 10 times.

This means that no matter how great somebody's willpower may be, if they are subjected to enough temptation over a long enough period of time, they will eventually give in. You can't run for 40 hours straight because you'll just run out of juice.

Psychologist Roy Baumeister of Case Western Reserve University conducted a study in 1996 measuring the phenomenon of what's known as *willpower depletion*. He gathered 67 study participants in a room with freshly baked cookies and other sweet confections, as well as some bitter radishes. Some lucky participants were allowed to indulge in the sweet treats, while the subjects in the experimental condition were asked to eat only the radishes—they had to exercise their willpower.

Unsurprisingly, the radish-eaters were less than pleased. Once they had been subjected to enough temptation as deemed by the research group, the participants went to a new location and were given a persistence-testing puzzle as a supposedly unrelated task. The effects of the forced willpower exercise were clear. The participants who had eaten only radishes made far fewer attempts at solving the puzzle and gave up in less than half the time relative to those who had been allowed to eat the sweets. Their willpower was depleted—*exhausted*—and they were ready to just take the path of least resistance.

The implications of the study are obvious. The subjects who were forced to resist the sweets had depleted their willpower in doing so, and so when they were asked to engage in another difficult task they were already worn out. It is a limited quantity, and while it can be drained, we must be careful with it, lest we fall prey to temptations with good timing.

Our brains have evolved over hundreds of thousands of years to make our daily survival the top priority. You know that you live in the modern age where temporarily low blood sugar and energy levels aren't likely to become life-threatening conditions, but your brain doesn't know that biologically. As a result, your brain is going to enter into survival mode. And survival mode is essentially a green light for instant gratification and binge eating, as well as a myriad of other failures of self-discipline.

To ensure that your willpower and self-discipline aren't exhausted, you'll be well served by making sure that you aren't challenging your willpower too strongly when you're hungry. Exercising your self-control can be beneficial, but ultimately the most effective way of maintaining discipline is by simply avoiding the situations that present the highest chances for failure. You might have the willpower to resist risking all of your hard-earned cash at the casino while you sit at the table, but then again, you might not. On the other hand, you'll certainly succeed in resisting that risk if you just don't go to the casino in the first place.

One other biological factor at play when it comes to willpower is stress. Whenever we are under a lot of stress, we are thrown back into our panicked "fight-or-flight" mode and are more likely to act instinctively and irrationally. Stress diverts energy away from the prefrontal cortex and causes us to focus more on short-term outcomes, which influences us to make regrettable decisions.

There are plenty of opportunities for you to conserve your willpower on a daily basis so you can prevent it from ever reaching dangerously depleted levels. All of those opportunities boil down to decreasing the amount of willpower you have to use by being smart about the decisions you have to make and being smart about the temptations you have to resist.

For example, let's say you have the incredibly common problem of sugar addiction. It's one of the easiest addictions to develop because sugar is hidden in just about all of our processed food items, and our prehistoric lizard brains still think that sugar and the energy it provides is a scarce resource that we should take advantage of whenever it is available.

Knowing that willpower isn't in unlimited supply, can you imagine how difficult it will be to resist those tasty snacks once you've brought them into your home? You might be able to do it the first few times the temptation pops into your mind, but it's practically inevitable that you'll give in to the temptation sooner or later. This is especially true if you place them in an area where you are continually exposed to them.

The better time to exercise some self-discipline, therefore, is at the grocery store. You can skip the aisles that have all of those unhealthy options so that you don't set yourself up for a failure of willpower later on. Rather than forcing yourself to avoid the temptation of going to your kitchen and grabbing an unhealthy snack, you avoid the temptation of buying that snack in the first place, meaning that instead of having to exercise your willpower indefinitely at home, you just have to manage it for 10 minutes at the store.

Meanwhile, you can optimize your self-discipline further by being smart about the decisions you have to make. In our same grocery shopping example, there will be a noticeable difference between trying to buy healthy items and avoiding the aisles with your biggest temptations if you are hungry versus after eating a filling meal. Here, you are making the choice to create conditions where you don't have to use self-discipline at vulnerable times. You are making the default action one that, while you may not love it, is what you would have chosen if you exercised self-discipline. This may not be a personal struggle for you, but surely the concept of trying to pick your battles wisely when it comes to discipline can be applied to just about all aspects of life.

Discipline itself is rather straightforward. You'll usually know the healthier or better option, and it's just a matter of choosing that option consistently even if the other options provide more immediate gratification. What can really make a difference for you is your *awareness* about discipline. The goal is to make it as easy as possible on yourself to be disciplined. You can best accomplish that goal by being aware of the factors that will fatigue your willpower and putting yourself into the most favorable circumstances possible.

Remember that discipline is biologically determined, and whether you consistently have it or you consistently fail to have it, that will become hardwired into your brain just like any other habit. Start by making it easier on yourself to exercise it and you'll likely begin having more success. The more you practice awareness about discipline and get in the habit of exercising your willpower, the stronger those functions will become. That's the path to sustainably increasing discipline in your daily life.

Takeaway: It may not be surprising that self-discipline has a biological basis. This means, like any of your muscles, it can be trained and also depleted and worn out. The latter is known as willpower fatigue. This is a good thing because it gives you a blueprint to deal with your self-discipline—you can increase it, and you can put yourself in situations to conserve it. It also means you can affect your self-discipline in positive ways through daily behaviors and habits.

Chapter 2. What Pushes Your Buttons?

Chapter 1 mentioned some of the most obvious scenarios where people need discipline, such as diet and exercise. In those cases, discipline isn't applied arbitrarily but rather for a specific purpose or set of reasons. Some behaviors are uninhibited, while a very specific set are controlled. Somebody who changes their diet or begins an exercise regimen is doing so because they want to feel and look healthier, fitter, and more attractive. There is a specific goal in mind, a specific outcome that is supposedly worth the work and willpower.

Knowing the exact outcome you want is an essential part of having self-discipline. You must be able to name it, describe it, and feel it. Otherwise, you're just forcing yourself into discomfort with the vague idea that you *should* be doing it. It's like marching in an army and not being sure whom you're going to fight or even why you're there.

It's impossible to maintain discipline without having a clear idea in your mind what you want to do. Of course, everybody is motivated by different things and in different ways, but there are some universal motivations we can consider. Finding the specific ways that you are motivated is paramount to accomplishing long-term goals, as it allows you more fuel to achieve; it's dangerous to rely solely on self-discipline and dragging yourself out of bed.

If we all had an infinite supply of motivation, maybe things like laziness, sloth, distractions, and temptations would cease to be problems. In reality, though, sustaining peak levels of motivation is a difficult proposition for even the most passionate of people. That's why it's important to pinpoint what drives you.

Discovering Motivation

Feeling motivated typically involves being excited about something. But unfortunately—for all but a lucky few—much of our daily lives must be devoted to doing things that aren't all that exciting. This might even apply to our jobs or careers. In those times, there can be immense benefits to figuring out what powerful motivators you have that you may not have realized yet about yourself. Remembering the "why" behind your actions keeps you grounded and gives you the fuel to push through difficulties. You can see this as the silver lining, or the reason that really gets you up in the morning.

It can be shocking to learn how much we misunderstand what motivates us. For instance, what motivates you in your job? You might be sorely mistaken. Psychologists Teresa Amabile and Steven Kramer illustrated our cluelessness in that regard.

After interviewing over 600 managers, an incredible 95% of them wrongly believed that their employees were most motivated by making money, getting bonuses, and earning promotions. Their entire workplace cultures were fundamentally flawed and weren't geared toward what the employees cared about. The real revelations came from the corresponding employees.

An in-depth analysis of more than 12,000 employee diary entries showed that the top motivator for workplace productivity wasn't financially or status driven. People were most incentivized to work by the feeling of making *consistent progress toward a meaningful goal*. The feeling that they were improving, getting better, and generally growing. Promises of bonuses, raises, and even recognition aren't going to make employees work harder; tying their work into self-development or an overarching goal will. It's one thing to be good at basketball, but to barely be able to dribble a ball and be able to dribble between your legs within a week is a far stronger motivator.

In case those 12,000 diary entries weren't evidence enough, another famous study by Dr. Edward Deci took a different approach to clarify what factor helps most with workplace engagement. Deci measured how long it took for the participants of his study to give up when given a difficult puzzle. Half the participants were placed in Group A and were offered a cash reward for solving the puzzle. The other half were in Group B, which wasn't offered a prize.

The first day of results went exactly as you would probably expect—Group A worked for almost twice as long at solving the puzzle as Group B. The next day, however, Deci told the Group A participants that there wouldn't be enough money to pay them to solve the puzzle this time around. Understandably, the participants in Group A weren't enthusiastic about the puzzle anymore and quickly gave up. Group B, meanwhile, worked for longer on the second day than on the first. In fact, Group B worked for increasingly more time in each successive session despite having never been offered money for their efforts.

On one hand, the study proves that money is a powerful short-term motivator. It's the lowest hanging fruit and most obvious cure for our problems and unhappiness. But at a certain point, it almost stops mattering. On the other hand, it seems that *being invested* in accomplishing a goal—in this case working on a puzzle for two consecutive days—proved to be more sustainable and effective in the long-term. When there's a challenge you want to overcome and surmount, it keeps you on your toes and keeps you motivated just for the sake of triumphing. Case in point: every single video game ever released.

These somewhat surprising results prompted the researchers to wonder what else impacts our work ethic and self-discipline. In addition to feelings of progress and investment, they have since come up with three main categories of motivation: autonomy, mastery, and purpose.

Our desire for autonomy means that we want to call our own shots and direct our own lives. Consider, for example, two young and imaginative students who are told to build a bridge out of Legos. If one is given an exact set of instructions to follow, and the other is allowed to design something original, which do you think will be more engaged in building the bridge? Probably the one who is allowed to follow their own vision and create something unique. Often the most beneficial way to help others be more productive and engaged is to simply get out of their way and let them pursue their own ideas while following their own intuition.

The second motivator, mastery, refers to our innate urge to get better at things. For an idea of how strongly mastery can impact our discipline, consider the legendary work ethic of Kobe Bryant. Whenever people would ask Kobe why he worked out at 4:00 a.m. or why he showed up to the gym to practice before anybody else arrived, he responded that he did it because he wanted to be the greatest basketball player he could possibly be.

Anybody who is highly driven by the idea of mastering their craft will be much more willing to make sacrifices and be disciplined in their pursuit than the typical person. Also—because truly mastering a craft is virtually impossible, there is a never-ending drive.

And then there's purpose—the feeling or intention that we can have an impact on the world. In many cases, discipline without purpose will probably just feel like pointless suffering. Somebody who doesn't feel called to help people who are sick or injured probably won't be as disciplined in medical school as somebody who does, for example. Desiring to live meaningfully and to contribute something useful to society is an integral part of being human. Someone who runs a charity will probably be imbued with greater motivation than someone who only contributes to the bank of them.

Which of these can you relate to and discover in your own life? Whatever it is you hope to accomplish, it will be an imperative part of your success that you can somehow put it into these three contexts of motivation. You can twist it however you like, but if your goal isn't somehow related to autonomy, mastery, or purpose, you're going to have a rough time in your pursuit of it.

Extrinsic versus Intrinsic Motivation

Though there are many types and flavors, all of your personal motivators will ultimately fall into two basic categories: extrinsic and intrinsic. Extrinsic motivation refers to that which depends on other people, environmental factors, or social factors. Intrinsic motivation, meanwhile, is dependent on the self and is based mostly on personal needs and wants.

Both kinds of motivation can be utilized effectively, but it's important to be honest in your assessment of which category your various motivations fall into. That awareness will determine how you reward yourself for good discipline and punish yourself when your discipline lapses. Namely, many people like to categorize themselves as having intrinsic motivators when they are almost exclusively extrinsically motivated.

Extrinsic motivators can also include pleasure-seeking, positive reinforcement, and even bribery. Our drives to accumulate wealth, reproduce, and achieve social status all fall into this category. This is when we do things for other people, rather than ourselves. They are the types of motivators that make us feel vulnerable to judgment.

We are also extrinsically motivated by avoiding suffering in the form of pain, fear, negative reinforcement, threats, and current unhappiness, among other things. Fear of financial instability can be a strong motivator to work hard and not get fired, while unhappiness with a job can be a strong motivator to spend a lot of time and energy looking for other options that might be more enjoyable. People generally want to be comfortable and happy as much as possible, but it often requires enough of one or more of these negative motivators to force us to be disciplined about making a change.

Yet the biggest extrinsic motivation is how we are perceived by others. Buddhist monks can dedicate immense amounts of their lives to learning how to *not* act as a result of their ego, pride, insecurity, or desire for power—but those things can be the driving forces behind our success in the material world. On a similar note, we also seek acceptance from our peers and may even conform socially to do so. For example, a young student whose classmates all play video games together online at night will be more motivated and disciplined about getting their homework done early enough to play than a student who doesn't have any interaction with their peers at night.

Considering the discipline and dedication it requires for monks to let go of extrinsic motivation, it's no surprise that there are plenty of people on the other side of the spectrum who use those motivators to maintain discipline in the pursuit of their goals. Being socially successful and highly viewed by others is enough to drive some people to accomplish truly amazing things. As long as you honestly recognize that about yourself and don't pretend to be someone you're not.

For many other people, success comes after letting go of extrinsic motivators and being introspective about intrinsic motivators—our personal needs and wants.

We all need food, water, and shelter for survival, as well as human connection for mental stability. If you're lacking in those things, everything else will take a back seat to your pursuit of the essentials for your survival.

After getting those basic needs taken care of, the next thing that we intrinsically desire is personal satisfaction and fulfillment. This might mean having work that is extremely interesting or has a positive impact on others, or being satisfied and fulfilled by personal relationships with friends and family members.

Satisfaction and fulfillment often come in the form of achievement, as well as personal growth and improvement. Some of the most disciplined people on the planet—world-class athletes—are likely motivated by both of these feelings as they put in the countless hours of practice and preparation required to compete at the highest level in their respective sports.

Ultimately, what's important in terms of discipline is simply that you are motivated and that you recognize those motivations. Maintaining discipline is impossible without having sufficient motivation, and likewise the achievement of intrinsic and extrinsic goals isn't possible without being disciplined.

Aristotle's Theory of Motivation

The famous philosopher Aristotle is credited with developing one of the original guides to human motivation. He created a work called the *Rhetoric* over the course of two time periods spent in Athens—first from 367 to 347 BC, and later from 335 to 322 BC.

In *Rhetoric*, Book 1, Chapter 10, Aristotle lays out his seven causes for human action. In summary, all actions are driven either emotionally or rationally. We seek pleasant things and act in order to reduce our pain and suffering.

The first cause for action that Aristotle mentions is **chance**. This refers to events that occur whose cause or purpose can't be determined and those that happen sporadically or seemingly randomly. For example, imagine how you might feel after encountering an old friend that you haven't seen in years and learning that they have become extremely successful. While you may be happy for them, it's possible that you'll still feel a bit of envy or regret. Those feelings can motivate you to pursue your own goals with a renewed enthusiasm and discipline. An event that had an incredibly low probability of occurring can serve as a life-changing catalyst given the right circumstances.

After chance, there are two subcategories for motivators that are not due to our own actions or chance, but rather necessity.

One subcategory of necessity motivators is **nature**—the things that have a fixed and internal cause, taking place relatively uniformly over time. It may be difficult to turn off Netflix while you're watching a really entertaining show, but you'll be motivated to exercise a little discipline and press the power button anyway. This is because you have a natural need to sleep and ignoring that need for too long will inevitably have negative health consequences.

The remaining necessity motivators that don't fall into the natural category are considered **compulsions**. A compulsion is an action that somebody feels motivated to take despite it being contrary to their desires or rationality. Somebody can want to be fit and healthy and understand that they need to eat well and exercise, but they might still feel compelled to eat an unhealthy meal or to skip a workout. It's something that has just lodged in their brain and they won't feel normal until they have partaken in it. It will typically require a good deal of self-discipline to consistently overcome compulsion.

Next, in a similar way as compulsions, **habits** can often be motivators that require a strong application of discipline to act in the way you desire. Forming a good habit, such as starting to practice meditation, will entail exercising discipline to build and maintain it until it becomes second nature.

Once a habit does become second nature, breaking it will be difficult, especially in the case of something like a drug addiction where you feel both physically and mentally compelled to continue the harmful behavior. Discipline in avoiding triggers and willpower in fighting off desires once they come will be necessary in overcoming any habit.

Then there are rational motivators developed through reasoning. These are the actions that appear to be constructive in achieving a goal or attaining something healthy and desirable. Being disciplined and studying hard in college isn't easy, but a student will be rationally motivated to do it if they know that it will help them get a job that they really desire.

Unfortunately, we aren't always able to be rational. Another two motivators for action are **anger and passion**, which stem from strong emotions and impulses. Somebody might, for example, be motivated to damage their own integrity in order to hurt somebody else in an emotionally charged moment. It would take discipline in your decision-making and awareness of thought patterns to overcome this potentially harmful urge.

Finally, the last of Aristotle's seven causes of action is our **appetite for pleasure**. After our basic needs are met, we can be irrationally driven by our desires in a way that motivates us to act against our own interests. You might go to the store to buy some essentials and find yourself with a cart full of things you don't need and didn't plan to spend money on, simply because you weren't disciplined enough to overcome your appetite for the pleasure of materialism.

Most people think of motivation only in the positive sense, believing that with a little more motivation they could work harder and be more successful. When it comes to discipline, though, motivation itself is neutral. Your understanding of what motivates you to act both positively and negatively will determine how effectively you can exercise discipline in order to achieve your goals.

It's up to you to be disciplined enough to avoid and resist negative motivators and to have a clear understanding of the positive motivators that can help you maintain self-discipline.

Takeaway: Self-discipline is important, but so is having a proper motivation to make self-discipline unnecessary. What you think might motivate you may not in reality, so it's important to be honest with yourself. Studies have consistently shown material possessions to be a poor motivator. Instead, personal feelings of progress, autonomy, mastery, and purpose are far better motivators to attach yourself to. Other factors include extrinsic versus intrinsic motivators and Aristotle's theory of motivation.

Chapter 3. Discipline Tactics of Navy SEALs

*Discipline equals freedom - Jocko Willink,
former NAVY Seal commander*

Whenever you want to push yourself to improve or achieve, you can turn to the veritable experts of that field.

In the case of self-discipline, the elite U.S. Navy unit, the SEALs, are truly the cream of the crop. SEAL stands for Sea, Air, and Land, and the individuals who become SEALs are famously skilled, disciplined, consistent, and capable. It requires extensive training to become a SEAL, and a vast majority of the soldiers who begin the training program don't make it through to the end. Those that do finish it embody the warrior archetype and epitomize the phrase "mind over matter." These men and women have the mental fortitude and physical toughness to accomplish whatever mission they are assigned and to persevere and endure extreme difficulties. Their very lives depend on it.

The 40% Rule

Maximizing human potential in the way that Navy SEALs push themselves to do has led to the development of a famous rule known as the 40% Rule.

The 40% Rule is straightforward. It says that when an individual's mind begins telling them that they are physically or emotionally maxed out, in reality they have only pushed themselves to 40% of their full capacity. In other words, they could endure 60% more if only they believed that they are capable of it. When you think you have reached your limits, you're not even close, and whether you can keep going or not depends on if you believe it. It's quite a belief to feel that you've reached your limits and say to yourself that you're only 40% done. It's an acceptance of pain.

We are usually ready to give up around the time that we begin to feel pain or are barely pressing our boundaries. But that point is actually just the beginning of what we are all capable of, and the key to unlocking more potential is to push through the initial pain and the self-doubt that surfaces along with it. By maintaining a belief in yourself, you show yourself that you can do more, and that evidence builds your confidence and mental toughness.

You might, for example, begin struggling after doing 10 push-ups. You'd start hearing the voice in your head that says you feel too tired, too sore, or too weak to go on. But if you take a pause and gather yourself to do one more, you find that you've already disproven the voice saying that you can't. Then you pause and do another. And then another.

And then another. Suddenly you're at 20. You can take it slowly, but you've just doubled what you thought was possible.

Believing that you can do more will make it true. It enables you to go well beyond the limits that you've constructed for yourself in your own mind. And once you've felt the pain and the urge to give up at 10 push-ups only to push through it and do 20, you know that your mental strength helped you persevere. The next time you're challenged, you'll feel all the more capable and prepared to push past your supposed limits again. This embodies self-discipline in a nutshell—it's really a matter of how much pain you can stomach, and most of us will only bend and never break.

Our minds can be our best friends when we have a strong belief in our capabilities, but they can also be a poisonous enemy if we allow negativity to seize control. It's up to you to empower yourself using the 40% Rule rather than throwing in the towel mentally at the first sign of resistance.

Imagine that you decide to run a 5k or even a full marathon despite being out of shape. Inevitably, as you run you'll begin to breathe harder, your legs will feel heavier, and you might question yourself. You could easily give up in that moment and save yourself from extra pain and soreness. But if circumstances were different and you were running away from danger out of self-preservation, you could undoubtedly continue on well beyond that first inclination to give in. Barring massive injuries, you'd finish if you believed the pain was part of the process. It's all a matter of whether you believe you can or not.

The reality is most of us have no clue about our true physical and mental limitations. Our lives are so much safer and more comfortable than those of our ancestors, and that has some undesirable consequences when it comes to mental strength. We don't test ourselves and we don't know what we're capable of. Now it is mostly the people who seek out intense challenges that subsequently learn discipline and mental strength, while the rest go about their comfortable lives without any idea of their full capabilities.

In case you're skeptical as to the merits of the 40% Rule, there is some scientific evidence in support of it that might help convince you. Numerous studies over the years have found that the placebo effect—the tangible change in performance caused merely by a belief that something you've done will impact performance—has a significant impact, especially in athletics. The legitimacy of the placebo effect suggests that your mental strength and toughness plays a big role in physical abilities. In other words, if you believe it, it will *be*.

One powerful demonstration of the placebo effect comes from a 2008 study published in the *European Journal of Neuroscience.* The study found that giving participants sugar pills and telling them that it was caffeine made them work significantly harder when they subsequently lifted weights. The belief that they would have extra strength and energy allowed the participants to tap further into their own potential without even being aware of it.

There is a scientific consensus that the placebo effect is not a deception, fluke, experimental bias, or statistical anomaly. Rather, it is a self-fulfilling prophecy in which the human brain anticipates an outcome and then produces that outcome of its own accord. In fact, the placebo effect closely follows the types of patterns you would expect to see if the brain was really producing its own desired results. Researchers have illustrated this phenomenon by showing that placebos follow the same dose-response curves as real medicines. Two pills give more relief than one, a larger pill has a stronger effect than a smaller one, and so on.

When you consider the placebo effect, it quickly becomes clear how powerful our minds are. Countless studies have supported the conclusion that the placebo effect is a result of chemical changes in the form of endorphin production. Just believing that you can give 60% more effort makes it possible.

Apart from athletic performance studies, the classic examples of the placebo effect are medical studies where people are given dummy pills but experience similar effects as the participants who were given the actual medications or vitamins. An interesting case is when people are given placebo painkillers and actually report alleviated pain. That the placebo effect can even impact pain suggests that any process controlled by our brains can be "tricked" by having a positive expectation.

So the placebo effect can obviously be used for performance enhancement, but how can it be applied to self-discipline?

Imagine how your odds of overcoming a strong addiction might change based on your attitude about that addiction. Believing that it's going to be hard and that you might not be capable will make failure a lot more likely than if you expect that you'll overcome the addiction. That's not to say that you should be naive and take a challenge lightly, but rather that you'll likely get the result that you expect to get.

For any goals that you have, struggles with discipline can probably be overcome by changing your expectations. The 40% Rule and the placebo effect both ultimately show that all of us are more capable than we give ourselves credit for. Whenever you find yourself making excuses or lacking discipline, consider those two phenomena and ask if your excuses are legitimate. Quite often, the underlying causes of lapses in discipline are the beliefs we create in our minds that we can't do something. Expecting yourself to be capable, successful, and disciplined will make it all the more likely that you actually are.

Arousal Control

As a result of hundreds of thousands of years of evolution, we have developed knee-jerk reactions and neurochemical responses to stimulation that are often highly undesirable when it comes to performing optimally. As mentioned in the previous chapter, the fight-or-flight response is one of these, which puts you into a state of massive physiological arousal and makes your mind go blank and necessarily lose all discipline and willpower in the interest of survival. These responses indeed contributed to increased chances of survival, but unfortunately, they don't have much of a place in modern society.

Being able to relax and focus in order to avoid distractions from natural stress responses is essential for self-discipline. Ordinary people simply can't control knee-jerk reactions such as shaking hands and sweaty palms because those reactions are caused by powerful hormones, including cortisol and adrenaline. We secrete hormones in large doses when we are under high stress or experiencing a good deal of fear, and controlling those secretions in the moment is next to impossible for us.

For Navy SEALs, however, succumbing to undesirable responses will mean the difference between life and death. As you might expect, they have some techniques that help them maintain clear mental states even in the most dangerous and stressful environments. One of those techniques that anybody can easily use is what's known as box breathing (Mark Divine).

This means that when SEALs recognize that they are feeling overwhelmed, they regain control by focusing on their breath—breathing in for four seconds, holding for four seconds, and then out for four seconds, and repeating until you can feel your heart rate slow down and normalize.

A stressed-out mind is an inefficient and uncreative mind, and so it is crucial for you to be able to remain calm if you want to perform to your full potential. Box breathing is simple to implement, and if it works for Navy SEALs, it can certainly work for us. The technique itself is easy, but the real key is to be able to recognize when your arousal might spiral out of control and sabotage your self-discipline.

Whenever you feel your heart beginning to race or your palms beginning to sweat, try focusing on your breath to reign in your undesirable reactions. If you can use box breathing at the first hint of physical arousal or stress, you will fare well because you will be able to control it. It's easier to stop it rather than manage it.

Meditation practices also often involve focusing on the breath and have a similar effect of reducing fight-or-flight instincts. However you go about it, controlling arousal can make a world of difference. Maybe it's the next time you're anxiously anticipating speaking in front of an audience, or perhaps taking an intense and important exam. Whatever it is that causes you stress, you'll be more adept to handle it with a clear mental state.

Bigger Goals Equal Better Results?

Does the ambitiousness of the goals you set change how likely you are to succeed? A substantial amount of research into that question suggests that it does.

In the New Directions in Goal-Setting Theory, Edwin A. Locke and Gary P. Latham notably stated, *"So long as a person is committed to the goal, has the requisite ability to attain it, and does not have conflicting goals, there is a positive, linear relationship between goal difficulty and task performance."*

To put it another way, setting challenging but realistic goals increases our performance in the pursuit of those goals. Modest goals don't inspire us in the same way as challenging ones, which results in an insufficient effort to achieve them. It's easy to see how this fits into the framework of the 40% Rule of Navy SEALs.

Suppose you'll be traveling abroad soon and you want to learn some of the local language beforehand. Scientific findings suggest that setting an ambitious goal like attaining an intermediate language level within a few months will be more likely to yield good results than a modest goal like just speaking the very basics. The time commitment for the former may be higher, but being adequately motivated to be disciplined in order to reach the goal is actually more likely for the bigger goal.

There's an even simpler rule, developed by Grant Cardone, that you can use to determine how loftily you set your goals. It's known as the 10X Rule, and it states that you should set targets that are 10 times more than what you think you want, and then take 10 times greater action than you think it is necessary to accomplish those targets.

The 10X Rule is over-the-top on purpose. The idea is to force you to change how you think about your own possibilities and how you plan to take action. You must realize that your thoughts and actions have brought you to your current place in life, and if you want to go further and achieve more you first have to start thinking and acting well beyond what you originally considered the norm. Ten times more than *anything* can seem shocking, but that just might be what's needed.

Take weight loss as an example. Say you want to lose 10 pounds, but after you apply the 10x Rule, you instead plan to lose 100 pounds. You may not even have 100 pounds to lose, but the point is in how your approach changes based on your goal. Losing 10 pounds might require diet and exercise changes for a few weeks, but you can easily fall back into old habits afterward. Losing 100 pounds, on the other hand, requires a complete lifestyle transformation that will take significantly more effort and discipline, but also yields sustainable, long-term results.

If you sit in a car for only 10 minutes, you won't prepare for the ride and may not even buckle your seatbelt. But how would you prepare for the car ride differently if you knew it was going to be 100 minutes long? You'd prepare music playlists, bring snacks, fill up the gas tank, and certainly wear your seatbelt.

The key is to stop selling yourself short. Believe that you are capable of more than you first thought, plan to achieve more, and then execute on that plan with discipline and effort. It's so common to set mediocre expectations for ourselves so that when we fail it's not such a letdown. But if you aren't willing to go after more, you'll always be stuck in mediocrity.

The 10-Minute Rule

Given our more developed brains, it's reasonable to think that humans are superior decision-makers to all the other primates of the world.

It's somewhat surprising, therefore, to learn about a famous experiment from Harvard University that tested discipline for humans versus chimpanzees. The critical part of the experiment came when researchers offered the same choice to both chimpanzees and humans—get two treats immediately or wait two minutes and get six treats. The chimpanzees chose to wait 72% of the time, while humans only chose to wait 19% of the time. Chimpanzees aren't smarter than us, so what is causing the counterintuitive discrepancy in good decision-making?

Well, the problem is actually in how developed our brains are. We overthink decisions with somewhat obvious answers and we are able to rationalize bad behavior that robs us of our more desirable outcomes. We're not always sure ourselves what's a real excuse and what's just a justification or excuse. You can imagine how this takes away from our overall efficacy.

That's where the 10-Minute Rule comes in—if you want something, wait at least 10 minutes before getting it. It's simple and leaves no room for debate or excuses. When you feel an urge, force yourself to wait for 10 minutes before giving in to whatever the urge is. If you're still craving it after 10 minutes, then have it. Or wait 10 more minutes because you've already done it and survived just fine. Simply by choosing to wait you remove the "immediate" from immediate gratification—building discipline and improving decision-making.

Similarly, if you want to quit something beneficial, wait just 10 more minutes. It's the same thought process applied in a different way. Ten minutes is nothing, so you can wait or continue that long easily. Then, if you do it once, it's easy to repeat, isn't it?

Another beneficial application of this thought process is the purposeful escalation of good habits. If you're doing something productive you might keep doing it for five minutes longer after you first feel the urge to quit. Then the following time you go for an extra six or seven minutes, and so on. Every time you feel distracted, just exercise discipline for a few minutes longer, and you'll steadily build better self-discipline with each escalation.

Being disciplined isn't easy. Quite often it requires using rationality to battle our instincts and natural reactions to stress. But even Navy SEALs, some of the most disciplined people on the planet, weren't born with focus and discipline built in.

SEALs build their discipline in a way that all of us can apply to our own lives. The intensity of their physical training instills in them the 40% Rule so that they are always able to push beyond their perceived limitations. They learn how to stay focused and calm in stressful circumstances so that they aren't susceptible to irrational lapses in discipline. And they are able to set lofty goals and execute plans to achieve those goals, avoiding the immediate gratifications and pitfalls along the way.

All of us are capable of living more disciplined lives; the SEALs merely provide a blueprint to make it happen.

Takeaway: Navy SEALs are routinely touted as masters of their willpower because it is the difference between life and death for them. They use a few tactics to keep taking action, the most well-known of which is the 40% Rule: when you think you've hit your limits, you're actually only at 40% capacity. Other tactics for discipline include box breathing for arousal control, setting big goals as a means to putting mind over matter, and the 10-Minute Rule.

Chapter 4. Diagnosing Discipline Drainers

Discipline is an essential skill to implement if you wish to accomplish your biggest goals and aspirations in life. Most people intuitively understand this, and yet most people are not nearly as disciplined as they need to be to reach their potential. Why is that the case? Are we all just in denial?

No, we all instinctually know what we need to do to improve and better ourselves. We all have the best of intentions. It's just that we get knocked off course more easily than we might realize. This chapter isn't meant to cast blame on external factors, but rather to bring awareness to the sneaky, covert ways that your self-discipline can be sabotaged. What is going on in your day-to-day life that prevents you from fully pursuing your goals and causes you to repeat negative behavior patterns? Lots.

Perhaps people in your social life are bad influences. You may also have negative thought patterns or harmful habits that you've developed without ever realizing the struggles they would cause you. You might have assumptions about your capacity for discipline, or the wrong set of motivations you are working toward. Whatever it is, you can certainly change it. This chapter will help with understanding and overcoming the discipline drainers that are holding you back.

False Hope Syndrome

One of the most common pitfalls in discipline is the belief that altering our behavioral patterns will be easy—this is known as the False Hope Syndrome. As a result of this belief, we tend to set unrealistically high expectations for ourselves that just guarantee that we will fail.

We routinely underestimate how difficult it is to break out of bad habits, and picture ourselves sailing through adversity as if it were an ideal world with no temptations. When we give ourselves too much false hope, we tend to fail more often than not, and often become more solidified in the behavior we wish to alter.

Psychology professor Peter Herman studies discipline and self-improvement and summarized why failure is so common even when we have solid intentions and motivation. He stated that many people tend to shoot for drastic and unsustainable changes, leading to inevitable failure. Being overly ambitious is often a result of underestimating the difficulty of achieving a goal or making a change.

You might have momentary clarity about your deepest desires and the path to attaining them, but when the stresses and difficulties of everyday life come in, that clarity fades away and is replaced by familiar temptations and pitfalls. In other words, the goals you find yourself working toward can easily take a back seat to emotional impulses that alleviate temporary discomfort—the exact things you don't account for.

Making significant changes and accomplishing big goals doesn't happen all at once. Continuing in that process typically requires positive feedback and tangible progress along the way, which you aren't likely to get if you've set unrealistic expectations for yourself.

Take smoking cigarettes—a habit that is both physically and psychologically addictive—for example. It's extremely difficult to quit cold turkey, yet when people try and fail to do so they will often feel discouraged and revert to previous levels of smoking. They are setting far too ambitious of a goal for themselves, and any slipup is tantamount to failure. They're putting themselves into a situation where they can't win.

What if, instead, people who wanted to quit started with a goal to cut smoking in half in the first month, then in half again in the second, and so on? After a few months, the urges would be much less frequent and the odds of successfully quitting entirely would be much greater—all because of a more attainable goal.

Successfully cutting back from 50 cigarettes per week to 25 over the course of a month is far more sustainable than immediately going from 50 to 0. Importantly, that progress provides consistent positive feedback to keep you motivated to continue. It also gives you the time to focus on your thought patterns and behaviors in order to develop new neural pathways in your brain so that you steadily change your habit.

The key is keeping your hopes for change grounded in reality and self-awareness. So how are you setting your goals for discipline and everything else? Are they an accurate reflection of your current capabilities, or are they based on the ideal version of you that will encounter no obstacles whatsoever? Avoiding false hope will be crucial to staying disciplined in your pursuits.

Thinking realistically about sustainability is every bit as important in self-discipline as motivation and inspiration. It may not make you as happy in the moment, and may even require you to seriously readjust your ego, but it will undoubtedly lead you to the outcome you want.

Procrastination versus Discipline

Procrastination is the enemy of self-discipline because it often means we are waiting for perfect conditions to justify inaction to ourselves. For instance, it's easy to postpone going to the gym because your calves are tired or it's raining outside. Just because the road isn't 100% clear for you to go to the gym doesn't mean you should forego it completely. They're just excuses.

What you should do to improve your self-discipline is simple. Stop waiting to "be ready" or for everything to feel "just right" before you begin pursuing your goals or changing your habits. Inaction goes hand-in-hand with making excuses and actually sabotages your chances of eventually being successful. When everything feels comfortable and just right, it's already too late and you've waited too long.

That may not immediately make sense to you, but consider why it's the case. If you make excuses and rationalizations now, what's going to stop you from making them in the future? When have you ever had the perfect circumstances in life, where it would be impossible for you to find some excuse or justification for more procrastination? If you're being honest, never.

Somebody who wants to give up smoking might decide to quit in a couple weeks because work will be less stressful then. But even that seemingly logical procrastination is detrimental because it can literally apply anytime and anywhere. Anytime you wait for circumstances to improve you're telling yourself that you aren't capable now. And that attitude isn't going to change when circumstances actually do improve—you'll just find another circumstance to hold you back.

You're always going to have doubts whenever you try to do something important. Taking on a challenge means that you'll be pulled in by the excitement of it but you'll also be pushed away by uncertainty. It's natural to wonder if you are prepared enough or qualified enough to do something difficult or to overcome an obstacle that you've never conquered before.

You can plan for the future and delay starting all you want, but the best thing you can do is to just start. It doesn't matter if that's getting healthy, writing a book, or starting a business— the best time to start is now. There is almost no perfect timing you should be waiting for. Waiting to have more money, resources, or experience very rarely increases your odds of accomplishing the goal in the future. You only have the chance to succeed once you've started, and you can always figure out the details along the way.

There's also the all too common myth in society that we should be striving for perfection. Again, this leads to procrastination because it creates a debilitating fear of failure—which prevents starting. When you recognize procrastination and the quest for perfection for what those things are—obstacles to being disciplined and successful—you give yourself the opportunity to act.

A healthy heuristic to combat procrastination and perfectionism is dubbed the 75% Rule. Simply, take action when you're only about 75% certain you'll be correct or successful. The truth is, you'll never be 100% certain, and typically when you're at 75% you are more than ready and even begin to have diminishing returns.

Thinking about discipline doesn't make you disciplined, as much as we may wish it would. Discipline only happens through consistent action. So when you're somewhere around that 75% threshold level, it's time to commit to your decisions and actions.

For example, suppose you want to run a marathon but you aren't very fit. The probability that you can safely run a full marathon is infinitesimal. But the probability that you can safely run two miles is substantially greater, perhaps around that 75% threshold. So that's where you'd start in your training. You might not feel ready for two miles, but you think you can probably do it, and the first step is always the most important.

After a little while, you might have a 75% probability of being able to run a half-marathon. Keep that up and you'll eventually have that same probability for the full marathon. Through this breakdown of a large goal into smaller ones, you make it realistic for yourself to start right away and to maintain discipline each step of the way without getting discouraged by failure.

If you're always afraid of failure or you allow your discipline to depend on external circumstances, you simply won't achieve the success you hope for. It takes a realistic approach and a willingness to act without certainty to build discipline.

Avoid Rationalizing

We all have a tendency to pat ourselves on the back for being disciplined in the past. While that can be rationalized as refreshing your willpower, showing yourself love, or just not being too rigid, the reality is that it often destroys much of the progress that you're rewarding yourself for building.

Our minds are constantly coming up with excuses to abandon discipline. One study started by asking people to recall a time when they were charitable and, after having done that, requesting that they make a charitable donation. Those who had thought about being charitable in the past donated 60% less per person than those who hadn't. That indicates that remembering having been charitable in the past made people less compelled to be charitable in the present, having already made themselves feel good or fulfilled their social obligation. In other words, they were able to rationalize out of donating because of past actions.

Simply thinking about the good they've done made them feel like they had done their duty, despite the fact that no further action had been taken. This is what will happen if you think about your past triumphs: you will associate those memories with the present, so it feels like you have nothing left to do. You will be able to rationalize undisciplined behavior, which undermines your goals.

The biggest obstacle is to recognize when it's happening and to hold yourself accountable. Regardless of how much you feel that you've earned a break or a reward for your past actions, accepting that tendency to rationalize or make excuses will have a negative impact on your discipline, plain and simple. Each moment or decision stands on its own and you don't get to "carry over" credit from past behavior. If you notice that you're using past actions to justify counterproductive actions in the present ("I was so good yesterday I can take a break today"), stop immediately and don't undercut your own progress. Each event should be taken in a vacuum, and you don't get an accumulation of points you can buy bad behavior with.

If you find yourself ever making statements such as "I did X, therefore I can Y," you know you have a tendency to rationalize!

Imagine that you're a recovering alcoholic who goes out to a restaurant to celebrate a friend's birthday. Rationalizations to have a drink would be easy—it's a birthday, why not celebrate? After several months of sobriety, one drink couldn't hurt. These are the victories you are calling on to justify undisciplined behavior. You see where this is going—after the first drink, you no longer have those months separating you from your last drink, so having a second drink is that much easier to justify. One lapse is all it takes.

An experiment at the University of Chicago further illustrated our tendency to self-rationalize lapses in discipline. Researchers recruited dieters and gave each one a congratulatory update on the progress they had made toward reaching their goal weight. Afterward, the participants were presented with a choice of either an apple or a chocolate bar as a reward. Eighty-five percent of the dieters who had been reminded of their progress chose the chocolate bar over the apple—after all, they rationalized, they'd earned it.

The moments when you catch yourself making excuses may actually be some of your best opportunities to exercise discipline. The dieters from the last study were doing well at resisting temptations and cravings when they were obvious, but their discipline fell short when it was challenged in a sneaky way. If you are aware of this tendency and you maintain your discipline in the face of it, you will be rewarded in two ways: you won't lose progress toward whatever goal that discipline is helping you to accomplish, and you'll strengthen your discipline by persevering through a difficult test.

Parkinson's Law

One of the things that people who procrastinate a lot might say to justify it is that they work better under a time crunch—"I work best with a deadline!" Interestingly, there is a law relating to discipline, known as Parkinson's Law, which validates that justification.

Parkinson's Law states that work expands so as to fill the time available for its completion. Whatever deadline you give yourself, big or small, that's how long you'll take to complete work. If you give yourself a relaxed deadline, you avoid being disciplined; if you give yourself a tight deadline, you can draw on your self-discipline.

The law was developed by a British historian named Cyril Parkinson, who initially noticed the trend while he was a part of the British Civil Service. He observed that as bureaucracies expanded, their efficiency decreased instead of increased. The more space and time people were given, the more they took—something that he realized was applicable to a wide range of other circumstances. The general form of the law became that increasing the size of something decreases its efficiency.

As it relates to discipline, Parkinson found that simple tasks would be made increasingly more complex in order to fill the time allotted to their completion. Decreasing the available time for completing a task caused that task to become simpler and easier and completed in a more timely fashion.

Very few people are ever going to require you or even ask you to work less. So if you want to be more productive and efficient, you'll have to avoid falling victim to Parkinson's Law yourself by applying artificial limitations on the time you give yourself to complete tasks. By simply giving yourself time limits and deadlines for your work, you force yourself to focus on the crucial elements of the task. You don't make things more complex or difficult than they need to be just to fill the time.

For example, say that your supervisor gives you a spreadsheet and asks you to make a few charts from it by the end of the week. The task might take an hour, but after looking over the spreadsheet you notice that it's disorganized and difficult to read, so you start editing it. This takes an entire week, but the charts you were supposed to generate would only have taken an hour. If you had been given the deadline of one day, you would have simply focused on the charts and ignored everything that wasn't important. When we are given the space, as Parkinson's Law dictates, we expand our work to fill the time.

Set aggressive deadlines so that you are actually challenging yourself on a consistent basis, and you'll avoid this pitfall. A long deadline also typically means a sustained level of background stress—push yourself to finish early and free your mind.

Diagnosing your discipline drainers may require you to analyze your actions closely. In what ways are you your own worst enemy? As you get a clearer picture of all the ways you might be self-sabotaging your discipline, don't forget that discipline is by nature unpleasant and difficult. You'll need realistic expectations so that you don't get exhausted or discouraged along the way.

Discipline is hard enough on its own—gain awareness of the ways you are making it harder on yourself than it needs to be.

Takeaway: A few common obstacles to discipline are setting your sights unrealistically high (False Hope Syndrome), procrastinating by striving for perfection (which can be combated by the 75% Rule), rationalizing excuses for inaction, and the effects of Parkinson's Law (which can be combated by setting aggressive deadlines).

Chapter 5. Flex Your "Uncomfortable Muscle"

Self-discipline is uncomfortable by nature. You would never willingly subject yourself to the struggle of being disciplined unless you had a strong purpose for doing so. We never hear about people needing discipline to eat ice cream or play video games.

There's no amount of knowledge, habit formation, thinking, or visualization that will make self-discipline comfortable. It's simply a fact that being disciplined is going to feel like a chore. The key quantity we need more of isn't necessarily always self-discipline itself—it's the amount of discomfort we can handle and tolerate. That endurance is what's meant by flexing your "uncomfortable muscle"—using mental toughness to power past instincts to choose what's easy, comfortable, and immediately gratifying.

This process seeks to turn a stabbing pain into a dull annoyance you can barely feel, or a hunger pang that you actually crave because it means you are sticking to your diet. Being disciplined comes down to choosing temporary discomfort that helps you in the long-term. Just as lifting weights causes temporary discomfort that allows muscles to grow back stronger, choosing disciplined actions and decision-making also makes your "uncomfortable muscle" stronger. Making a regular habit of embracing uncomfortable situations can have a positive impact on all aspects of your life.

Shifting your view of discomfort and choosing to embrace it equips you with the mental strength to thrive regardless of whatever difficulties, temptations, and failures you experience. Discipline doesn't care if you are exhausted, irritated, or even dejected—that's when you need it the most. Exercising discipline quite literally trains your brain to default to a mode of perseverance.

Urge Surfing

Developing discipline is tough, but there are some accepted methodologies for making it *easier* by understanding how to reduce the strength of urges and temptations. Urges are defined as impulses to engage in a habitual behavior or past addiction, and they are frequently manifested in physical sensations in the body, not just in thoughts.

The late psychologist Alan Marlatt, a pioneer in the field of addiction treatment, developed a methodology for dealing with urges. Marlatt's technique is appropriately called *urge surfing*, where urges are compared to ocean waves that you surf over as they rise in intensity, peak, and then eventually crash.

Urge surfing can be thought of as an exercise for training your self-discipline and mental toughness. It's meant to teach you how to embrace discomfort and resist temptations.

The next section will give a more detailed explanation of urge surfing, but here is a basic set of instructions so that you can understand what urge surfing is before moving on: Pause whatever you are doing for a moment and think about an urge that you recently felt. Whatever the urge was, think about it and pay attention to the physical and emotional sensations experienced with it. Indulge in it. Notice how these sensations evolve over time. As you're doing this, softly focus on your breath to help you ride out the urges, imagining that they are waves and you are surfing across them.

Our natural tendency is to identify with our urges, and urge surfing helps us to separate our identity from whatever past habits and tendencies we want to correct. Instead of thinking, *I want a cigarette,* you might think, *I have an urge to have a cigarette*. It's not a part of you that you must fight, but rather a **sensation** that you experience, observe, and then let pass or settle. Fighting urges is rarely effective, but curiously observing urges without identifying with them gives you much greater odds to overcome them.

A typical urge will peak between 20 and 30 minutes *if you battle it.* Battling urges, or trying to get rid of them, is counterproductive as it usually makes them stronger and longer-lasting. Furthermore, battling an urge makes it that much more deeply ingrained while simultaneously weakening your confidence in your ability to change it in the future. But when you choose an open attitude about your urges and watch them without fighting them, they subside much more quickly and effortlessly.

The power of urges comes from your willingness to indulge them, not from the addictions and temptations themselves. This point is illustrated well by patients at rehab facilities, who find that being entirely cut off from any access to addictive substances results in remarkably few cravings and urges compared to what they would experience outside. These facilities remove their patients' internal struggles, without which there is nothing to feed the urges. Thus, they simply pass by.

You may not be able to check yourself into a rehab facility in order to remove the internal struggle from your quest to be disciplined, but that is all the more reason to practice urge surfing.

Another useful metaphor for this internal struggle is to think of the urges as a waterfall, where battling the urges is equivalent to trying to block the waterfall. Of course, it's inevitable that the waterfall will break through, perhaps even more forcefully than it originally was because of the pressure built up by trying to block it. Mindfulness is the escape from this impossible scenario because rather than trying to block the waterfall, or urge, you step away from it and just watch it. This strategy is crucial to identify, as implementing it is one of the most effective ways to improve self-efficacy.

If you can successfully change your attitude about urges and temptations to one of curiosity instead of fear or resignation, you'll also be able to change your behavior. Scientifically study your own habits. But as long as you fight your urges, you're setting yourself up for failure. In learning to accept and observe them, you make it possible to watch them quickly fade away.

Are You Unintentionally Feeding Your Urges?

After realizing that fighting urges is a losing battle, you might logically think that you should try to intervene earlier on in the process. This can be done by distracting yourself or trying to think your way out of an urge.

Similarly to fighting urges, however, distractions and rationalizations have the opposite result of what you desire. These techniques actually feed urges and make them stronger while also building an illusion in your mind that urges won't go away until you succumb to them. When fighting urges *and* distracting yourself from them both inevitably fail, it's understandable that you might feel defeated. Many people reach this stage and surrender to the idea that they aren't capable of changing bad habits.

Distracting yourself from urges may not logically seem like something that harms discipline. Many people think of distractions as a sort of self-created rehab center, where you reduce urges by reducing your opportunities to indulge them. Unfortunately, it just doesn't work that way in real life. In fact, there have been numerous studies in the last several decades showing that suppressing thoughts, feelings, and sensations ultimately makes them stronger (Clark Ball & Pape 1991; Gold & Wegner 1995; Wegner, Schneider, Carter & White, 1987; Wegner, Schneider, Knutson & McMahon 1991; Cioffi & Holloway 1993).

This phenomenon is easily illustrated through a psychological game that you've probably experienced before. The game is simply to try to not think of something in particular after somebody mentions it. Somebody might say, for example, "Whatever you do, do not think about a hippopotamus." Of course, each subsequent mention of hippopotamuses will make not thinking about them all the more impossible. Actually, the harder you try to avoid that thought, the more it consumes you. And so it is with trying to avoid urges.

That's not to say that distractions and battling with urges never works—sometimes it does. But even in those cases, the battle leaves you feeling irritable and annoyed rather than relaxed and calm. You aren't going to be able to trick your own mind and feel positive about it in the process, as much as you may try.

We are only interested in effective and sustainable solutions. In the case of overcoming urges, that solution is surfing the urge. In learning to be disciplined, you become comfortable with the discomfort of seeing an urge and not indulging it. It's far more comfortable to judge our urges and to view them as the enemy, but this mindset will always acknowledge the urges we want to eliminate.

The next time you feel an urge and you are ready to implement the urge surfing technique, follow these steps:

1. Take a few moments to notice where in your body you are experiencing the urges. Just as hearing music might give you an urge to tap your feet or bob your head, most urges can actually be felt in the body if we have awareness.
2. Once you connect the urge to the place in your body that it's felt most strongly, focus your attention on that area. Observe the sensations you have there.
3. Spend 1–2 minutes noticing your breath.
4. Imagine that the sensations you feel as a result of your urge are a wave. Watch that wave rising and falling as your urge peaks and subsides.
5. As the urge inevitably passes, take note of its transient nature. The next time an urge arises, you'll be that much more confident in your ability to ride it out to its conclusion.

What's important to take away from this experience is that everything you think and feel is temporary, including desires. When you forget that fact, cravings and urges can feel overwhelming. But if you are patient and confident in your ability to ride out a temporary urge until it passes, you will find that it's far more effective than trying to distract yourself or battle the urges head-on.

When you get the first pangs of hunger in your stomach, you might think that it won't go away until you have something to eat. Hunger is also one of the urges that most commonly causes irritability, as being productive when you're hungry is extremely difficult. But as anybody who has experimented with fasting knows, hunger is as temporary as any other urge.

You might notice that you feel hungry when you are bored or when you've been sitting for a while at work. You might feel the pangs in your stomach, but if you pay attention closely you don't feel that your stomach is empty or that you are in dire need of calories to energize yourself. A few minutes of just accepting the hunger and not taking it as a strict sign that you need to eat can actually make that hunger quickly fade away. Hunger pangs go away and don't mean you're going to starve or faint.

Start taking an interest in your urges and studying or experimenting with them. You'll learn that you are not the urges you feel until you fight them or succumb to them. As long as you simply observe them coming and going, they lose much of their power to negatively influence your behavior.

Practice Discomfort

You may recall from the first chapter that willpower is like a muscle that fatigues the more you use it within a given time. This is actually good news, because willpower fatiguing like a muscle means that it can be strengthened like one, too.

The "exercise" that most effectively increases your baseline level of willpower is leaving your comfort zone. That involves pushing yourself to regularly do things that you aren't completely comfortable doing so that you become familiar with the feeling of discomfort itself. Leaving your comfort zone is important because it teaches you that the things you fear aren't as bad as they might seem. Each time you learn that lesson in some small way, your tolerance for discomfort and your willpower both increase.

You don't need to be uncomfortable in your daily life, but being familiar with the feeling sure helps you in the face of actual adversity. You can even create anxiety and uncertainty yourself—so that they are controlled and manageable—to show yourself that you are capable of handling it.

Jia Jiang gave a popular TED Talk about his personal journey outside of his comfort zone, in which he confronted his fear of rejection and the social anxiety that came with it. Jiang wanted to become more confident, so he set out to desensitize himself to rejection by seeking rejection out in some small and controlled way 100 days in a row. Some of Jiang's rejections included borrowing $100 from a stranger, requesting a "burger refill," and asking to play soccer in somebody's backyard. When the 100 days were up, Jiang was a new person with more confidence and a greater appreciation for how kind people are to one another.

Jiang's story of overcoming a fear of rejection is applicable to everybody. Your personal fears and discomforts are also your opportunities to challenge yourself. If you like to be in control, spend a day deferring to other people. If you're more comfortable being passive, spend a day asserting yourself and making more decisions. Whatever you are comfortable doing—do the opposite.

Injecting manageable discomfort and uncertainty into your life isn't difficult to do. You might order the dish on the restaurant menu that has ingredients you haven't heard of before. Or instead of taking a relaxing, hot shower, you could turn the water to cold and force yourself to stand in it until you gain control of your breath and calm your mind. Ask people for discounts that you don't think you'll get. Sit down in a restaurant and then leave after receiving the menu—that walk to the door will feel incredibly long.

Even just doing something spontaneous or out of character can get you out of your comfort zone enough to see that your uncomfortable zone isn't that bad. If you are clumsy and awkward and you don't like dancing, go to a dance class. The worst thing that can happen is a few other people at a beginner's class learning that you are bad at dancing—and they certainly won't care. Your willingness to even try will probably endear you to others, quite the opposite of the embarrassment and isolation that you might fear.

Discipline is inherently uncomfortable, so improving your relationship with discomfort is one of the best ways to improve self-discipline. Everybody has different fears, insecurities, and discomforts. But a lot of people go through their life avoiding those things, and thus limiting their own potential. If you want to maximize all of the positive aspects of your life, you can start with facing your fears and choosing to be uncomfortable.

As this practice builds your willpower, you can begin to change some of your less beneficial habits and addictions. When you feel pulled into a battle with your urges, you'll have the mental strength to resist that temptation and to instead ride the urges out like a wave. And if fear motivates you to avoid your urges altogether by distracting yourself from them, fear is sometimes an opportunity for positive change.

Discomfort and struggle are what make you who you are. You're reading this book because you want to be more disciplined, so if you're going to follow through on that, then it's time for you to get comfortable with discomfort.

Takeaway: Self-discipline is in itself an act of discomfort, so it makes sense to practice discomfort like a muscle. One of the most effective ways to practice discomfort is to "surf the urge" which has been shown to be better than actively resisting urges. Further, you can practice rejection therapy or simply put yourself in uncomfortable situations, mostly social, that will require you to act.

Chapter 6. Creating A Disciplined Environment

There is more to being disciplined than the obvious factors of mental strength and willpower. One of the biggest influencers of self-discipline is the environment in which you're implementing it. Environmental factors can either enable discipline or weaken it, and it's unlikely that it will play no role at all.

Knowing that your environment affects your success, why play with fire? Designing and maintaining an environment that's conducive to self-discipline is one of the simplest ways that you can drastically improve your life. As important as it is to exercise your willpower and build it up, the most desirable environment is one in which you rarely even need to rely on willpower at all—your desired action or outcome simply occurs because that is one of the only choices.

Conserving your willpower is about removing the distractions and temptations that knock you off course. We all understand this when it's obvious—you wouldn't go into an Italian restaurant known for its homemade pasta if you're trying to avoid carbs, for example. You're bound to have more success with losing weight if you live in a gym versus living in an ice cream factory. But there may be some less obvious ways that you can improve the ways that environmental factors are influencing your self-discipline, which is what this chapter is all about.

Testing and depleting your willpower when it's not necessary should be avoided as much as possible. Designing the optimal environment is more than half the battle.

Minimizing Distractions

We often think that distractions can be our friends when it comes to self-discipline. If willpower is finite, then we reason that it's better to take a break, refresh, and distract ourselves from urges and temptations.

Baba Shiv, a professor of marketing at the Stanford Graduate School of Business, conducted a study that illustrates how distractions affect us. Shiv distracted one group of participants by asking them to remember a phone number and then asked all the study participants to choose either chocolate cake or fruit. Those who were trying to remember phone numbers chose the cake 50% more often than those who weren't. The conclusion here is that focus is an essential part of being disciplined.

If you're constantly distracted, you succumb to temptations without even giving yourself a chance to exercise your willpower. It just doesn't occur to you, and you choose the path of least resistance despite your best intentions. Distractions sneakily eat away at our self-discipline. This process can go on in the background so that we don't even realize that our discipline is lapsing until it's too late and all of our past efforts have been wasted.

The design of checkout lanes in supermarkets is a prime example of capitalizing on distracted minds and depleted willpower. You can make healthy decisions every step of the way through the grocery store, but you can't escape without one final distraction of candy, chocolate, and snacks at the register. This is frequently the most difficult time to be disciplined because you're so close to exiting and thinking ahead and the items are cheap and available to purchase instantly.

What should you do with this knowledge? If you work in a cluttered environment, clean it up. A clean desk can help create a clear mind, and a clear mind is much more able to remain disciplined. A Cornell University study provides some compelling evidence supporting the concept of "*out of sight, out of mind*" as a means of improving discipline, and it applies to far more beyond your desk.

The study participants were given a jar full of Hershey's Kisses that was either clear or opaque, and either placed on their desk or six feet away. On average, the participants ate 7.7 Kisses per day from the clear jars on their desks as opposed to 4.6 per day from opaque jars in the same location. When the jars were placed six feet away, the participants ate 5.6 Kisses per day from the clear jars and 3.1 per day from the opaque jars.

Surprisingly, the study subjects consistently reported feeling that they had eaten more Kisses when the jars were placed six feet away, even though the opposite was true. That discrepancy is a crucial piece of information because it provides a simple guideline for improving discipline. That is, you can use laziness to your advantage by clearing your workplace of distractions. You may not completely forget about those distractions, but the more effort it takes for you to give in to a temptation, the less likely you are to do so. Furthermore, it eliminates some of the most counterproductive discipline lapses—the mindless ones that we don't even realize we are doing.

It's so much easier to reach your hand into a cookie jar without thinking about it if that jar is easily accessible and visible. Those are the types of scenarios that you want to avoid when designing an environment for discipline. If you place the cookie jar in a distant cabinet, you don't eliminate the temptation altogether but you make it so that giving in to the temptation requires a lot of effort. That makes a big difference.

Ultimately, you want to create an environment for yourself that is clear of distractions and obvious temptations. You can make discipline drastically easier just by eliminating the mindless and effortless lapses in discipline that are made possible by an environment that hasn't been optimized. This applies to your desk, your workspace, your office, what you can see from your desk, and even your computer desktop. Keep them clear of distractions as much as possible and you'll simply forget about them. In your lapses of discipline or boredom, you'll have no other option than to keep working.

Regulate Dopamine

Whenever we are experiencing pleasure, a hormone called dopamine is released in our brains. As you probably know, dopamine is commonly associated with sex, drugs, and rock n' roll—all the things that we humans enjoy. Dopamine makes us feel happy and our brains learn to like the activities that cause dopamine releases. Naturally, we like feeling good, so we often set aside our other priorities to subtly seek out more dopamine.

That can be a good thing for healthy habits that induce dopamine releases such as exercising, meditating, or reducing sugar intake. But it can also be extremely harmful—especially in the world of modern technology and social media. In fact, we are practically wading around in the stuff now, as everything from processed foods to Internet pornography is profitable because of its ability to become addictive through tapping into our dopamine reward system.

If you aren't aware of the harms of constant dopamine hits or you do nothing to reduce them, you'll often be distracted by a pervasive urge to get more of it. Something as simple as checking who's liked your last post on social media can quickly develop into an irresistible itch to constantly refresh your feeds. Much of your daily life will be spent thoughtlessly seeking little pleasures and, at the same time, ignoring the things you're supposed to be doing. A covert dopamine addiction can be the downfall of your discipline and productivity.

A series of famous behavioral psychology studies, first conducted by psychologist B. F. Skinner, showed that dopamine is a fundamental part of habit formation—good and bad. Skinner and the psychologists who built off his work observed many interesting behavioral phenomena in rats. It was shown that rats who were missing dopamine receptors struggled to build habits. On the opposite extreme, rats that were given a lever to directly stimulate their brains' dopamine receptors pressed the levers thousands of times in an hour, choosing dopamine over food, water, sex, and childcare. In fact, the rats would have kept pressing the levers until they died if the scientists had let them.

For humans, dopamine releases are caused by more than just pleasure—it's also a result of anticipating pleasure. We can easily get bored by predictability, but novel rewards keep us on edge and elicit stronger dopamine responses. That's a big part of the reason that behavior gets so strongly reinforced, as the strength of the dopamine release correlates to the desire to repeat the behavior that caused it. Dangerous drugs like heroin are an obvious example of this, as some people can become addicted to them after only a single use because of how strongly they impact dopamine.

How does this manifest in our lives today? Social media interaction—likes, comments, messages, and even just scrolling through a feed all give us little dopamine hits. Many social media platforms profit from "time on site," meaning the amount of time users spend on their platform. As a result, those platforms have been optimized to tap into dopamine responses as much as possible, because addicted users are profitable ones.

It's important to be informed about all of these battles going on to tap into our dopamine systems and to limit their effectiveness on us. Building an environment that insulates you from these dopamine hits is important.

But you can also use the brain's reward center for your own purposes: create rewards for yourself for positive behavior so that you actually reinforce the habits you want instead of being addicted to small dopamine hits that take you away from your day. Obviously this will involve imposing limits on social media.

Drug rehab facilities use a kind of lottery game called the fish bowl to take advantage of novel rewards leading to reinforced behavior (Petry, 2003). Patients who have stuck to their regimens and avoided relapsing all get to reach into the fish bowl and draw out a slip. One might have a big prize such as $100 and others may have smaller prizes like $10 or even $1.

Most won't have a financial prize, but will just say something such as, "You're doing great! Keep up the good work!" This system has been shown to work quite well, with one study finding that patients who participated in the fish bowl game completed the rehab course in 83% of cases, while only 20% of those who didn't participate completed the course.

You can create your own fish bowl to reinforce good habits and decisions. It might mean pairing an activity that you need to do but don't enjoy with some sort of reward, even as small as a slip of paper drawn randomly from a hat. If you struggle to find the motivation to exercise, it can make a big difference to schedule a time to exercise with a friend. You associate the exercise with the reward of getting to socialize with somebody you like, and as a result, you look forward to going to the gym.

Think about all the ways you are pulled toward rabbit holes for dopamine in your daily life, and try to use those things to your advantage however possible. If you're going to eat snacks at work, try having them only after you've reached a milestone or completed a significant task. Use small, incremental rewards to reinforce good habits and you'll see improvements in your behavior and self-discipline as a result.

Default to Positive Actions and Behaviors

Optimizing your environment for self-discipline really comes down to understanding how automatic most of your decision-making is.

To illustrate that point, consider the findings of a study conducted in 11 European countries on organ donors. The data showed that countries who automatically have citizens opted-in to being organ donors—requiring action to opt-out—had rates at or above 95% participation. When the default choice was not to be an organ donor, however, the highest rate found in any of the 11 countries was a mere 27% participation. Ultimately, people just went with the option that required the least effort. It said nothing about their actual intention or desire to be an organ donor.

This same concept of defaulting to the more desirable choice can be applied to your own self-discipline. We're lazy and will happily accept whatever is in front of our faces. You can make it easy for yourself to choose whichever options most benefit you while also making it as difficult as possible to make harmful decisions.

A default option is one that the decision-maker chooses if he or she does nothing, or the minimal amount of effort. In other contexts, default options also include those that are normative or suggested. Countless experiments and observational studies have shown that making an option the default will increase the likelihood of it being chosen, which is known as the default effect. Making decisions requires energy, so we often choose the default option to conserve energy and avoid making decisions, especially when we aren't familiar with what it is we are making a decision about.

Optimizing these default decisions is where the bulk of your efforts to make a more discipline-conducive environment can take place. You might believe that you control the majority of your choices, but in reality, that isn't the case. Instead, a significant amount of your actions are just responses to your environment.

If you're distracted by social media, for example, you might move the app icons to the back page of your phone so that you aren't constantly seeing them whenever you open your phone to do something else. Better yet, you can log out of the apps after each use or delete them from your phone altogether so that you'll only use them when you really want to instead of letting them be distractions.

And if you're in the habit of mindlessly picking up your phone while working, you can simply start placing it faced down and far enough away that you have to get up to reach it. If you want to practice violin more, put it on your desk with your music notes open. If you want to floss your teeth more, keep floss in your backpack, in your bathroom, on your night stand, and on your sofa.

There is a seemingly endless number of examples of how you can utilize the default effect to become more disciplined with very little use of willpower itself. Another one is that leaving potato chips and cookies out on the kitchen counter will make it your default choice to eat those things whenever you walk to the kitchen feeling even the slightest bit hungry. Hiding those (or not buying them at all) and replacing those unhealthy snacks with fruit will instantly increase the probability that you eat fruit and that you avoid the unhealthy snacks. Want to exercise more? Put a pull-up bar in your bathroom doorway.

If you keep sugary sodas and juices in your refrigerator, you're making it your default choice to drink them whenever you are thirsty and open the fridge. But if you don't have those options, you increase the likelihood that you'll drink water, or make tea. Want to take more vitamins? Put them right next to your toothbrush for easier access.

If you sit in an office all day and have back problems, then you might benefit from standing up and walking frequently throughout the day. You can make this your default option by drinking water constantly so that you are forced to get up to go to the bathroom. Or perhaps you could schedule alarms on your phone and place it somewhere out of reach so that you have to stand up to turn off the alarm whenever it goes off.

The whole point of this is that you can save your willpower and your energy by making positive changes to your environment. The two biggest facets of environmental change are reducing clutter and distractions and optimizing choices based on the default effect.

If you reduce distractions from your environment, you'll clear your mind, which in turn increases focus, efficiency, and productivity. Furthermore, you can use your dopamine reward system to your advantage by reinforcing your own good habits while also cutting back on mindless pursuits of small pleasures. Finally, you can make it so the path with the least effort leads to the choices you desire and benefit from.

These all make it so you can sidestep actually using discipline and to save it for your bigger daily challenges. After all, why exercise willpower when you don't need to if you can plan around it?

Takeaway: The environments you create for yourself has a huge impact on your self-discipline because it can either constantly drain it, or it can help you conserve and exercise it. You should strategically limit your distractions by employing "out of sight, out of mind," minimize dopamine spikes that sabotage your focus, and make the path of least resistance the action you want the most.

Chapter 7. The Relationships That Inform Our Willpower

You'll notice a similar theme from the previous chapter here—we may not truly control our decisions or discipline as much as we might like to think. Most of us go through life thinking that we are fully capable of making decisions for ourselves. Many of our decisions, we believe, are based on what we think of as common sense, while others derive from our unique experiences and perspective.

A large body of evidence exists, however, that indicates that in fact we often do not make decisions on our own; rather, our decisions are significantly influenced by the people around us. You can call it peer pressure, social expectations, or just the desire to conform. Whatever it is, our relationships are a very real foundation of our self-discipline for better or worse.

A study known as the Asch conformity experiments provided compelling evidence of how we are influenced by those around us. In a group setting, subjects were given a vision test with one extremely obvious correct answer. The first several respondents were planted by the researchers and had been instructed to give the same incorrect answer. This differed from the correct answer. And yet, upon seeing the results of the cohorts, over one-third of the "real" subjects ended up giving the same incorrect answer. They abandoned their own common sense and perspective to conform with the others.

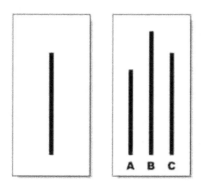

Courtesy of Simplypsychology.com

As you can see, there was no reason except pressure to conform for people to change their minds. Something that seemed so obvious was put into doubt when others disagreed, which made people think, "What am I not seeing?" People didn't want to feel stupid or ostracized, so they conformed despite hard evidence staring them in the face.

Longer-term evidence comes from the Framingham Heart Study, which tracked subjects for a period of 54 years. The results were dramatic. The odds that participants in the study became obese increased by 171% if they had an obese friend. A woman with an obese sister had a 67% higher risk of obesity. Similarly, a man with an obese brother had a 45% higher risk of obesity. If we can look past the fact that there were likely some genetic factors, we find that people simply fall into the same life habits and patterns of the people around them. They form an ecosystem where certain actions fit and are compatible, and others don't. Hopefully for you, this ecosystem is full of healthy behavioral patterns and self-discipline.

The people we surround ourselves with, whether intentionally or not (no one choose their family), significantly influence our self-discipline and decision-making. It may be a surprise as to how much you think you're acting out of free will when you're just emulating what you see around you.

Invest in Your Network

We can't choose our families, but we can certainly choose whom we spend our free time with. We should be selective in the people we associate with. We can't change our families but we can adjust how much time we spend with them, particularly if we are fortunate enough to recognize when they provide an unhealthy influence. Apart from family it becomes clear that we must choose our friends wisely. This allows us to leverage the same dynamic—the influence that those close to us have on our decisions—in a positive direction.

Brain scan studies have shown that the same part of our brain is activated when we think of our mothers as when we think of ourselves. Our brains, it seems, see others the same way they see ourselves—at least close relatives or friends. This provides a clear explanation for why behavior can be so contagious. When those others do something, we literally feel ourselves engaging in it, and manifest the urge to do it, too. Think of the implications: other people are influencing what we do, how we think, who we are! Again, that's good news if it is a positive action but bad news if it is negative.

In many cases social pressure drives behavior. We know of the examples of teens doing dumb things because of peer pressure. But it can be a positive influence as well. It is commonly utilized by organizations such as sports teams and the military. People feel a sense of loyalty to their teammates and don't want to hold them back, so they give maximum effort. A deeply felt sense of loyalty, whether to people, country, or principles, can be a powerful source of self-discipline.

You may have heard it said that you are the average of the five people you spend the most time with. We know that to the brain we are the same as those close to us. It is an almost logical conclusion that your perspective is only one-sixth of what determines your actions, behaviors, and habits. The rest depends on others. Armed with this insight, what can we do to improve our daily behavior?

Not just for self-discipline, fill your network with people that you admire and whom you look up to—not those whom you look down upon and whom you have to prop up. If you find yourself in a room and you are the most accomplished person, or any other relevant superlative, it's time to find a new room.

Whatever you feel your weaknesses are, you can surely find people with those as strengths. You can also make sure to befriend people who are generally positive and supportive in your endeavors, so no matter what, they are a force of good in your life.

Accountability Partners

Aside from creating better relationships around you, you can focus on one person whom you might essentially report to. They keep you accountable and try to make sure you keep your commitments and are on track to hit your goals.

The University of Pittsburgh conducted a weight-loss intervention that required participants to bring a friend or family member who also needed to lose weight. One group within the study was given "support homework," where the partners were told to praise and encourage each other. Successful examples of self-discipline involving food and exercise were to be celebrated. This is known as having an "accountability partner." The other group in the study had no such "homework." Ten months after the end of the program, 66% of the participants in the group that provided support and encouragement to their partners had maintained their weight loss. Only 24% from the other group were able to do so.

It was concluded that it wasn't necessarily emphasizing the victories that cemented the weight loss, it was having a supportive presence that gave people mental and emotional resilience.

Having an accountability partner can be a powerful way to help both of you achieve a challenging goal. It combines the elements that influence behavior, including the social pressure of not wanting to let your teammates down, and the way your brain wants to emulate those around you. The key is giving and receiving a constant stream of positive support: encouragement, celebration, praise. To earn the praise, however, you must continue to deliver the effort. You become more invested and put forth more effort if you know you have the possibility of disappointing multiple people.

Running a marathon is among the most difficult physical challenges to overcome. One of the keys to preparation is simply getting out there and logging the miles. How easy it would be when the alarm goes off on a cold early morning to just roll over and tell yourself it's okay to skip this one day and that you'll make it up next time. Now imagine your running buddy is going to be there waiting for you at your starting point. Will you really leave her hanging?

And keep in mind that the expectation that *you* will be there is a primary motivator for your buddy to get out of bed! Together you will achieve great things. Even if your running buddy isn't with you every day, what about someone that checks in with you daily about your morning run? It's just another safeguard to keep you in line. To be specific, an accountability partner works only when you communicate constantly about the work that's been put in and when you capitalize on the feelings of togetherness and not wanting to let others down.

Can solely telling other people about your goal be a useful variation to having an accountability partner? You may think it provides sufficient social pressure to keep you on your plan, such as publicly announcing your New Year's Eve resolutions. In fact, *telling* people of your goals makes them less likely to be achieved!

When you tell people your goal—to lose 25 pounds, to run a marathon—you will typically receive praise and congratulations. Way to go! But this tricks you into thinking you have actually achieved something already, like the act of telling people has fulfilled your duties. This has the adverse effect of *reducing* your willpower and self-discipline. People who tell others of their goal lose their drive and are less likely to achieve it. It may be that having your goal acknowledged makes it a part of your identity and provides that rush of feel-good reward hormones.

NYU Professor Peter Gollwitzer specializes in how goals affect behavior. He conducted four studies involving 63 subjects and found that those who kept their goals private were more likely to achieve them than those who told people about them and had them acknowledged. He concluded that telling others of your goals gives you a "premature sense of completeness." The way this works is based on the "identity symbols" in your brain that give you your self-image. These symbols in your brain can be created both by talk and action. As a result, *talking* about your goals creates similar symbols to the *actions* required to achieve them. Your brain now has its symbol and "neglects the pursuit of further symbols."

A related study found that when a goal has sub-components, success in one of the sub-goals can reduce efforts on the others. For example, to improve your health you may be determined to eat more healthily and hit the gym more often. Yet success at healthy eating can reduce your motivation to work out. You may rationalize to yourself that you had a salad for lunch, so you can skip tonight's workout.

Your overall goal is to improve your health and your healthy eating is giving your brain the symbol it wants.

What does all this mean?

As much as you want to talk about them, you are better off keeping your goals private. However, involve people in the process of your goal and the actions toward them. If you do happen to tell anyone, make sure you do not do it in a way that elicits praise. Quite the opposite. Tell them of your dissatisfaction with your current state and that they should kick your butt if they see you straying from your plan.

Telling an accountability partner is even better. You won't get any praise or congratulations from your accountability partner until you have actually done something to earn it. And the ongoing social pressure to keep going and not let your partner down will provide your brain with the motivation you need. Think of that cold morning when you are deciding whether to get out of bed for a 15-mile run. Which will be a stronger motivator: the fact that you told someone about your goal weeks ago or the fact that your shivering friend will be out there waiting for you?

The Hawthorne Effect

Research has shown that another way people's behavior is influenced is when they have the feeling of being watched. Back in the 1930s, the Hawthorne Works Electric Company was trying to understand the drivers of productivity. They thought they were on to something when they found that worker output soared when the lights were turned up. Then they noticed that turning the lights *down* had the same outcome. They were baffled.

Analyzing the data 20 years later, Henry Landsberger discovered what he called the Hawthorne Effect. Landsberger realized that it wasn't the lighting at all. What was actually influencing the behavior of the workers was the awareness that they were being observed. The employees worked harder when they saw they were under scrutiny, which was indicated to them because the lights were continually being adjusted.

We can take advantage of this principle by making our behavior more observable. One example is running and activity apps such as Runkeeper and Fitbit, which not only track your runs, your mileage, or your steps, but also post them where they can be seen by your friends. It's like having virtual running buddies. They are watching to be sure you are doing what you should be doing, and you don't want to let them down.

Or suppose you are cutting back on carbs in order to lose weight. Let your friends and coworkers know that you are giving up pizza, bagels, and soda. Include them all on an email chain where you send them a link to a chart of your daily calories or exercise quantity. Just knowing they are keeping an eye on you will be a powerful motivator to maintain your self-discipline. It makes you self-conscious.

It comes down to this: would you pick your nose if someone was watching? No. Keeping yourself monitored in whatever way possible can make it so you aren't depending on self-discipline per se, but social pressure and shame.

Keeping people in the loop thus puts them in a position to keep tabs on you, and the knowledge that you are being watched will keep you on track. So spread the word while being sure to let people know that you are expecting them to hold you accountable. And don't let them congratulate you simply for setting a goal.

Role Models

A final way to ensure a positive influence from those around you is to seek out a role model or a mentor.

This is a person you admire and look up to, a person who displays the types of behaviors you wish to emulate. It may not be as hard as you think to establish such a relationship. People are flattered to be told they are seen as a role model and will usually make time for you. You don't even need to make a formal agreement, or any type of agreement at all. As long as you have someone to actively look up to, you will be passively improving yourself.

Even if you don't have a role model in real life, piecing together an image of your ideal role model is a helpful exercise that provides clarity on what you are seeking. Moreover, it helps you visualize difficult circumstances by simply asking what your role model might do in that situation.

We may think of role models as most appropriate for kids but there is no age limit. Adults can, and should, have role models. We experience new challenges at every stage of our lives. Learning from people who've been there, who have handled it successfully, is invaluable. It's also the most efficient means of learning because instead of fumbling and struggling by yourself, you have someone to give personalized advice according to your unique perspective.

You can gain an entirely different view by listening to your mentor talk about their successes and failures, how they maintain their self-discipline, and how they solve problems. You will realize there is more than one way to deal with different situations. And you will probably identify behaviors in yourself that are holding you back, are self-defeating. The best role model will also act as a mirror—they will allow you to gain more self-awareness about how you are by contrasting how they act in certain situations.

The traits and behaviors that make your role model successful will work for you. You admire their dedication, discipline, self-confidence, compassion, courage, positive outlook. Copy them, mimic them. Qualities and habits can be learned, and they will make you a stronger, more disciplined person.

How you choose to conduct your personal life is, of course, up to you. But there remains powerful evidence that strategically surrounding yourself with supporters, challengers, and role models can have a marked benefit on your life. You can even think of it as a personal board of supervisors. Not everyone can help you on everything, but you're bound to have at least one helpful opinion or perspective on any challenge you face.

Takeaway: More than our environments, we are perhaps most influenced by the relationships we keep. Our social circle informs us as to what is acceptable, can support us, or can hold us back. You can't choose your family, but you can choose whom you spend your time with, as well as proactively seek out mentors and role models to shore up your weaknesses.

Chapter 8. Why You Should Always Eat Your Vegetables First

In other words, the art of delayed gratification.

Choosing long-term benefits over short-term pleasure is at the heart of a self-disciplined lifestyle. You're limiting your immediate pleasure in exchange for an even greater future pleasure. Taking on challenges and tolerating unpleasant feelings that we usually try to avoid are often crucial aspects of delaying gratification.

In fact, delayed gratification is another way you can define self-discipline because it takes you through the same process to the same outcome. You suffer now for a specific outcome later, and it requires mental fortitude, pushing your boundaries, and doing more than you thought you could. Whenever you seek to delay gratification, you use self-discipline. They are inseparable concepts.

This chapter will explain how to consciously start thinking about your future self—the one you are delaying gratification and suffering for.

The Stanford Marshmallow Experiment

Delaying gratification is a more than a behavior; it's a skill—something that was best demonstrated by a famous study known as the Stanford Marshmallow Experiment that was referred to in the very first chapter of the book. It's such a seminal study that you can probably mention "the marshmallow study" and people will know what you are referring to.

Psychologist Walter Mischel first organized the study in the 1960s, but what made it truly significant was the findings of continued observation of the study participants for some 40 years afterward.

The original experiment was simple. The researcher would give the participant—a child—one marshmallow. Then the child would be presented with a choice: eat the marshmallow now, or wait for a while and earn a bonus marshmallow for their patience. The researchers left the room for roughly 15 minutes to let the children ruminate and make their decision. The ones who chose to wait and delay gratification for the two marshmallows happened to be the children that scored higher on academic metrics and personality questionnaires. In other words, there was an extremely high correlation between the ability to delay gratification and high performance.

Dr. Mischel and his team then followed the participants as they grew up from preschoolers into young adulthood, carefully tracking information about their successes and failures and general performance in life. They discovered that those participants who had delayed gratification in the marshmallow experiment when they were younger went on to have higher SAT scores, lower levels of substance abuse, lower levels of obesity, healthier stress management, better focus, and higher achievement in a variety of other metrics relative to the participants who hadn't delayed gratification.

Another interesting finding was that the parents of children who had delayed gratification reported that they were more competent than instant gratifiers despite not knowing how their children had performed in the experiment. Over the following 40 years, the group who had waited patiently to earn a second marshmallow succeeded time and time again in whatever capacity they were measured.

The Stanford Marshmallow Experiment and the data collected following it prove that being able to delay gratification is a crucial life skill in order to be successful. It might be one of the foundational skills that underlie high achievement. We have to be willing to purposefully delay positive events and rewards until after we've completed some objectives or achieved some goals. Sure, it might make sense to do the easy things first in order to overcome inertia and create positive momentum when we are struggling to get going. But when you choose to do the difficult things first, you give yourself greater incentive to follow through to completion and to maintain discipline along the way.

Think about your daily life and all of the improvements that delaying gratification can make.

You might put off watching the latest episode of your favorite TV show until after finishing your homework, for example. That incentivizes you to focus more and to work more efficiently, which might lead to improved learning and better grades. It will also allow you to properly enjoy Seinfeld reruns without the specter of homework stressing you out.

Delaying the gratification of finishing your workout until you get through a few more difficult reps can lead to significant gains in strength and mental toughness. You can delay the gratification of quitting during a tough run in the quest for better fitness. After leaving the gym, you can delay the gratification of eating something quick and unhealthy in order to go home and prepare a nutritious meal.

Unfortunately, the payoffs in real life are rarely so immediate or tangible. Often, we're delaying our gratification in longer and grander ways such as going to medical school and finally reaping the rewards in your mid-30s, or buying a used car to save money to buy a house in a few years. Yet it is still the same process of exercising self-discipline in making that choice.

Being good at delaying gratification makes you better at just about every feat of discipline you can think of, which happens to be necessary to excel in any field or skill. What most people lack, and why they fail at self-discipline, is having a clear and compelling payoff that they are suffering for.

You start by knowing your values and what is important to you. Recall in the chapter on motivations that they may not be what you would like to assume. You could be driven by social impact like Mother Teresa, or you could be driven by pure money like Gordon Gecko. What's important is that you know which it is for yourself and keep your short-term and long-term payoffs constantly in mind. You can also design rewards around them.

The longer you stick with your positive behaviors the easier and more natural they'll become. If you're used to eating your dessert first, it's a shock to the system to begin with your vegetables, but worth it in the long-term.

Act on Behalf of Your Future Self

Struggling with discipline can be seen as struggling to put your future well-being ahead of your current happiness or pleasure. One explanation for why so many people experience those struggles is the inability to relate or connect to our future selves. In fact, research has indicated that simply imagining your future self more vividly can have a positive impact on self-discipline.

A Stanford University study by Hal Ersner-Hershfield and a team of collaborators used functional magnetitic resonance imaging (fMRI) technology in order to observe what happens in the brain when we think about our future selves. Subjects were asked to describe themselves in the present and 10 years into the future, as well as to describe other people. The neural patterns evoked when people thought about themselves 10 years into the future were consistently most similar to the neural patterns evoked by thinking about other people.

In other words, we have an emotional disconnect from the person we are going to become many years from now. We don't seem to care about our future selves and thus won't act in their best interests.

Being disconnected from our future selves helps explain many behaviors that could be considered failures of discipline. People who aren't concerned about their future self aren't going to be motivated to save enough for retirement, for example. It also explains why somebody might continue indulging in behaviors like eating an unhealthy diet despite being aware that they are risking incurring diseases and other health issues as a result. Other things like acting without integrity and failing to make sound ethical decisions likewise are easier to understand, as those concepts are less important to somebody who isn't concerned about their future.

All that is to say that viewing our future self as if it's another person doesn't have a positive effect on us. Significantly, the study participants whose brain images most strongly indicated that they viewed their future selves like another person were also the ones who exercised the least patience in making a financial decision during another exercise of the study. That means that there was a correlation between seeing the future self as another person and being unable to delay gratification—in this case, to earn a greater financial reward than the initial offer.

It is going to be extremely difficult to make plans for the future and execute them with discipline if you aren't able to delay gratification. For the majority of people, current problems and pleasures are a lot more important than anything that's going to happen in the future. So how can we go about fixing the mental disconnect that we have with our future selves?

Getting people to think long-term has been a big dilemma for psychologists, but they have discovered something that makes a difference. It comes down to visualizing exactly who you are, who you will be, and who you want to be. That helps to create a tangible connection to your future self, which makes it significantly more likely that you'll act on that future self's behalf.

The same psychologist from the earlier fMRI study, Dr. Ersner-Hershfield, conducted another experiment attempting to learn how he could increase people's inclinations to delay gratification. Before the experiment began, he took pictures of the participants and used software to create digital avatars of them. Half of the participants had avatars of their current selves, while the avatars for the other half were aged with jowls, bags under the eyes, and gray hair.

The subjects then explored virtual environments as their avatars, eventually coming to a mirror reflecting either their current or future self. Following the virtual reality experience, participants were asked how they would allocate $1,000 given four options—buying a gift for somebody special, investing in a retirement fund, planning a fun event, or depositing the money into a checking account. Those that had seen an aged version of themselves reflected in the virtual mirror put nearly double the amount of money into the retirement fund as the other participants.

As an experimental control, the researchers also tested how people would respond after seeing older avatars of other subjects. They found, however, that only the participants who saw their own future selves favored long-term options more than those who saw their present selves. In other words, the tangible visualization of your future self makes that future self seem much less like a stranger. As a result of that visualization, people are much more likely to make decisions that are better for them in the long-term.

If you want to have a similar experience to the participants who were shown aged versions of themselves, you can actually go online and search for facial aging apps or software that will return plenty of free options. This can be a very powerful tool for delaying gratification and discipline in general because it helps you to care about your future self more than you would without that visualization. But this step isn't necessary.

A more practical application of the study's findings is just thinking of your future self experiencing the consequences of your present self's actions more often. For example, imagine that you are tempted to procrastinate on work. Rather than giving in to that temptation, you could think about your future self not doing the work and missing out on opportunities to socialize and have fun or just relax without stress because your present self wants to be lazy. Put yourself in the shoes of your future self with as much detail as possible. Think about how much you'll suffer and how what the real cost-benefit of your lack of discipline is.

It's easy to say you'll do something later when you don't actually think about it, but once you do you give yourself the opportunity to be disciplined. At that point, the right decision will usually be obvious and even feel easier.

The 10-10-10 Rule

No matter how well you visualize your future self or how skilled you become at delaying gratification, you'll still inevitably face temptations or urges to lose discipline that can overcome you. If that means being less rigorous about your diet for one meal while you're out with friends, it's probably not a big deal. But if that means that you're about to lose your willpower and relapse on a harmful addiction of the past, you'll want to have a tool up your sleeve to help you stay disciplined. That's where the 10-10-10 Rule comes in.

The next time you feel that you're about to give in to an urge or temptation, stop and ask yourself how you will feel 10 minutes, 10 hours, and 10 days from now. The 10-10-10 Rule may not seem all that powerful, but it's effective because it forces you to think about your future self and to see how your actions are going to affect yourself in the future—for better or worse. A lot of times, we know that we are losing discipline or doing something harmful in the moment, but that's not enough to stop us from doing it because we don't have any connection to our future self that will have to deal with the consequences. The 10-10-10 Rule quickly creates that connection, and that can make the difference between a success or failure of discipline.

Why time intervals of 10 minutes, hours, and days? Because that helps you realize how short-term the pleasure or comfort of a discipline is relative to its long-term consequences. At 10 minutes, you might be feeling good, with perhaps just the initial bit of shame creeping in. After 10 hours, you'll feel mostly shame a regret. Ten days later, you might be consumed by regret having realized some of the negative consequences that your decision or action has had on your pursuit of your long-term goals.

On the other hand, you might apply the 10-10-10 Rule and realize that a lapse in discipline now won't make a difference 10 days into the future. If that's the case, then you can indulge a bit without guilt or shame.

For example, imagine that you apply the 10-10-10 Rule when deciding whether or not to skip a workout to go to dinner with coworkers. If you've just begun exercising and haven't built it into a consistent habit yet, your decision to skip a single workout might increase the odds of skipping future workouts or stopping working out altogether.

How will you feel in 10 minutes, hours, and days? Ten minutes—good, with a slight tinge of regret, as you can still taste the lasagna or ice cream. The pleasure is still tangible. Ten hours—almost entirely regret, as the pleasure is gone and fleeting, and your diet has been soundly broken. Ten days—100% regret, because the broken discipline is now completely meaningless and but a faint memory.

On the other hand, if exercising is already a consistent and enjoyable habit for you, then imagining how you'll feel 10 days from now will quickly show you that one skipped workout isn't harmful to your long-term discipline or goals.

And when you're not swayed by the 10-10-10 Rule or your dilemma of willpower is extra difficult, you can add a final question for yourself. That is, how will breaking willpower now affect you in 10 weeks or even longer-term? You might want to change the parameters to 10 weeks if you're mostly engaged in longer-term decisions and tasks.

In this process, it's obviously crucial to be honest with yourself and wary of your own abilities to rationalize and make excuses. For example, you may have tried to quit an addictive habit many times in the past, only to fail and eventually reinforce the harmful behavior. If you have a history of falling into bad habits after a single lapse in discipline, then an honest assessment of how you would feel after 10 days or 10 weeks will tell you that you simply can't afford a lapse in discipline now if you're going to achieve your long-term goals. It wasn't an exception or justified in that one circumstance—it is a reflection of your character for better or worse.

Without that honesty and ability to see your own rationalizing and excuses for what they are, applying the 10-10-10 Rule may be a futile exercise.

In general, getting better at delaying gratification goes hand-in-hand with greater self-discipline. The more vividly you can visualize and relate to your future self, the more likely you are to delay gratification in moments of temptation, so you should explore ways of creating a more solid connection to your future self. You can start by saving the best for last on your dinner plate, and really relish those last few bites that you've saved for yourself. And when delaying gratification isn't that simple or easy, you can pause and use the 10-10-10 Rule to make the healthiest decision possible—starting with your vegetables, of course.

Takeaway: The concept of delayed gratification is not new. It's the ability to eat your vegetables before you to eat your dessert. Studies have found that this simple ability is highly correlated with high performance in various aspects of life. Another way to look at it is to proactively think about your future self more—the one who will be rewarded for your temporary suffering. Finally, you can take a peek into the future with the 10-10-10 Rule: how will you feel or be affected 10 minutes, 10 hours, and 10 days after choosing a lapse in self-discipline?

Chapter 9. Quick! Read in Case of Temptation!

Discipline is never easy. At best, it's like wearing wet socks over a long period of time. You know it's unpleasant and you don't prefer it, but you're so used to it that you don't necessarily mind so long as it doesn't get much worse. You're still wearing wet socks at the end of the day.

But sometimes trying to be disciplined is overwhelmingly difficult. It can make you want to break down or tear your hair out at the brink of frustration or exhaustion. Luckily, there is a set of questions you can ask yourself to get back on track. The questions are intended to

return your focus to your goals and pursuits—
the things that motivate you to be disciplined
in the first place. They might also shed light on
your real reasons for wanting to persist or quit,
which can be illuminating.

If you make the effort to ask yourself these
four questions and to be honest in your
answers, you'll become more aware of your
tendencies to rationalize and make excuses
and you'll be prepared to create better habits
for leading a disciplined life.

Question 1

The first question you should ask yourself is the
most straightforward. It forces you to classify
yourself in either a harsh or positive light.

Do I want to be a disciplined person or not?

Don't give yourself any wiggle room in how you
answer this question—it should be a simple yes
or no. If you stop or quit, you must answer a no.
There are no exceptions, ifs, ands, or buts.
Either you are disciplined or you aren't; there

isn't any space in between. If you are disciplined, you'll do the thing you don't feel like doing because that's what is necessary to pursue your goals. You must classify yourself one way or another at each juncture.

Of course, reality isn't black and white. One lapse in discipline doesn't make you an undisciplined person; it just makes you human. But when you approach a decision or action as if it is that black or white, it provides strong motivation against failure because you don't want to view yourself as somebody who doesn't have discipline. Any other course of action is failure when there is no gray area. You are forced to consider if you are okay with being defined in that way, or if you want to rise above it and maintain discipline even when you aren't feeling great.

You'll obviously want to be able to answer yes—that you are disciplined. Since there is no way to answer yes and to then have a lapse in discipline, you'll feel compelled to follow through and make the right decision.

Imagine you have work to do, but you feel tired so you want to put it off and relax instead. The more time you spend analyzing that decision, the more opportunity you are giving yourself to rationalize being lazy. If left unchecked, your mind would quickly convince you that there's nothing wrong with procrastinating until you are less tired or the work is more urgent. But if you make the decision black or white, you know that one action is disciplined and the other isn't. You nip this thought process in the bud and spring yourself into action because you won't want to see yourself as an undisciplined person.

At that point, you can't lie to yourself or rationalize acting without discipline. If you choose not to start working, that is clear evidence that you are a person without discipline in the pursuit of your goals. Sometimes taking a simple approach gives us the push we need to avoid a failure of self-discipline. It also has the bonus effect of shaming you into action.

Question 2

The second question to ask yourself when your discipline is feeling shaky can further prevent harmful rationalizations. The smarter you are, the easier it is to fool yourself. Therefore, trying to truly understand why you want to break discipline is important.

Am I doing the right thing or simply what's easy?

Very often, doing the right thing means doing the hard thing. Unfortunately, they are frequently the exact same thing. The average person doesn't typically choose things that are difficult when there is an alternative, which is why discipline is often the missing component for many people who don't fulfill their goals. People tend to drift toward the path of least resistance, consciously or not. If you don't want that to be you, you'll need to be able to accurately answer whether you are doing what's right or not.

When you can't confidently say that you're doing the right thing, you are forced to see how you are making excuses for yourself.

That's an important step because you aren't going to build discipline and accomplish your goals if you buy into your own rationalizations and excuses. If you're not doing what you should be, then anything else out of your mouth is an excuse, plain and simple.

You've probably experienced when you were invited to a social engagement you didn't want to attend. Sometimes in that situation, we will struggle to come up with excuses for not going that won't offend whoever invited us. We do it because we think it's less rude or confrontational than just stating the truth— that we don't want to go. Yet we often fail to recognize when we are doing the exact same thing to ourselves in order to feel better. It would actually be better to start being honest and upfront with yourself about your behavior.

Instead of rationalizing skipping a run because "it's too hot outside" or "it's too late," you would just start saying, "I'm not going to run today because I'm too soft and lazy to maintain discipline."

In reality, why are you skipping the run? Because you're lazy. You know the right thing to do is run. Therefore, you are taking the easy way out. There's no wiggle room here, just like the first question of the chapter. You'll begin to realize the excuses and rationalizations that you usually make. In effect, you become brutally honest and confrontational with yourself, which can make a difference and lead to a change in behavior.

You should always want to answer that you're doing what's right, and that will frequently mean that you have to make a little extra effort. But when you do it consistently, that extra effort pays off.

For example, you might have the opportunity to cheat while taking an exam. Knowing that they wouldn't be caught, the typical student probably takes that opportunity to cheat and runs with it. But then the final exam comes around, and now the test-taking environment is much more closely monitored to the point that cheating would be risky or even impossible. The students who didn't cheat on previous exams and relied on their own studying will have actually learned the material throughout the semester and given themselves a good shot at success, while the students who cheated their way through the entire semester won't know anything on the final exam.

Reaching your goals isn't all that different from succeeding on that final exam. Sure, you might find little successes from shortcuts from rationalizations along the way, but eventually it catches up to you and you'll find you don't have what it takes. Doing the right thing may feel like the harder route in the moment, but when you do it consistently it winds up being the most efficient route to accomplishing your goals.

Question 3

Without goals and aspirations, discipline is going to feel like pointless suffering. Therefore, our lapses in discipline often come when we aren't connected to our goals. That's where the third question comes in. It brings clarity to what you are trying to accomplish and the entire reason you are suffering or exercising uncomfortable discipline.

These are the vegetables, so what am I getting for dessert?

Essentially, you're being disciplined and taking on discomfort now so that you can experience some personal benefit in the future. The disciplined behavior is the vegetables, and the payoff is the dessert. It's easy to falter if you forget what your payoff is.

If you lose sight of your goals or the reward that you'll eventually earn by being disciplined, your discipline will fail because, as mentioned, you'll feel like you are engaging in pointless suffering. Not having a clear idea of what you're working toward will make you feel like you simply shouldn't bother.

We lose sight of the dessert in two main ways.

First, we forget it. This is why it's extremely important to keep reminders in easily accessible places and to be constantly recalling the *why* that makes discipline both necessary and worthwhile. Pictures, alarms, and cues of every flavor to make your future rewards as tangible as possible.

Second, the dessert isn't compelling by itself and hasn't been tied into something sufficiently motivating. If your dessert or reward isn't significant enough to justify the temporary discomfort you experience by being disciplined, it will be that much harder to stay with it. You have to know exactly what that reward that you're pursuing is, and ideally, it should be something that you think and care about on a daily basis. You should also extrapolate how it contributes to your life on a grander scale and all the benefits you will receive from it.

Bodybuilders are an example of truly suffering for their payoff. They must rigorously maintain a healthy diet and consistent exercise regimen for months in advance of a bodybuilding competition. Then, the week before the competition, they cut their food intake to a fraction and work even harder. It's truly suffering on a physical, mental, and emotional level.

Yet they persist year after year because they feel that their payoff is worthwhile. They feel that their suffering is worthwhile for the amount of life impact and benefits their physique can bring them. They have the possibility to literally become millionaires from endorsements, triumph over competition, reach the pinnacle of their sport, and become legends. The suffering is worth the potential payoff to them, and they are reminded of it on a daily basis to stay on track.

So ask yourself, what am I really doing all of this for? You probably don't have such extreme discipline requirements as a bodybuilder, but you should ensure that your payoff is salient and truly moves you. The more discipline you require of yourself, the greater your reward must be at the finish line. Regardless of the ambitiousness of your goals, reminding yourself of them on a consistent basis will make you understand the necessity of discipline and stick with it.

Question 4

Have you ever given in to an urge without even realizing that you were doing it in the moment? For most of us, that answer is yes, which is why we have the last question of our series of failure-prevention questions. If we can accomplish the most difficult of tasks, thinking about our thinking, we can more successfully tame our impulses and act disciplined.

Am I being self-aware?

Don't feel bad about lapses in self-awareness; they happen to everyone. As you know, however, distractions and impulses are the enemy of discipline. Studies have shown that people who are distracted while grocery shopping are more likely to eat food samples and make impulse purchases than more aware shoppers. And why wouldn't they be? Thinking logically with a distracted mind is impossible, so it's not a good bet that you'll make the right decision in those instances.

Self-awareness is important enough to make or break your self-discipline. If your mind is always wandering away from the present, you'll find that you don't even know when your discipline is lapsing until it's too late. Not only that, but your "why" from the third question is of no use. You want to reduce things like stress, fear, and anxiety as much as possible in order to stay present and clear-minded in your daily life.

Of course, meditation has been shown to be a viable method of achieving that state of present awareness. Really, anything that you can do that gets you to focus on the present is a good thing—whether that's creating art, listening to music, or playing a sport. Anything that creates more self-awareness in your daily life will ultimately help with self-discipline.

Of course, just by remembering to ask these questions, you are being self-aware in some way. But honestly answering yes to that last question also means that you aren't giving in to temptations or feeding them.

For example, somebody who is addicted to pornography might be doing well to avoid it, but then come across an arousing picture on social media that triggers their addictive habit. Being self-aware in that moment means that as soon as the person feels their response to the image, they recognize that feeding that response at all will make it harder to be disciplined. Instead of mindlessly staying on social media and looking at more pictures until the urge becomes stronger, having self-awareness helps to cut it off at a manageable place. You may not be able to catch yourself in the act, but being self-aware means at least catching yourself earlier and earlier in the process, as opposed to sitting for an hour on social media and then wondering where the time went.

Our brains simply seek hedonic pleasure the vast majority of the time, and with increased self-awareness, you can examine the patterns and behaviors that can lead you down negative paths.

Any one of the four questions from this chapter on its own can be helpful enough to prevent a lapse in discipline. The fact that you're reading this book means that you want to be disciplined, so asking yourself if your actions reflect that you are disciplined is a good first step. Further questioning whether you're doing what's right or taking the easy road really forces you to confront any tendencies you have to rationalize and make excuses. Consistently reminding yourself of your goals and motivations fosters a strong sense of the importance of being disciplined. Finally, self-awareness pulls it all together and helps you to stay focused and clear-minded in your disciplined pursuits.

Question yourself, be honest in how you respond, and watch as your habits of discipline grow stronger and stronger in the process.

Takeaway: There are four broad and illuminating questions to immediately ask yourself in the face of any temptation, distraction, or impulse. Are you disciplined or not? Are you doing the easy thing or what's right? What are you getting for dessert? Are you being self-aware?

Chapter 10. Mindset and Approach Are Everything

Your mindset profoundly affects how positively or negatively you perceive your life and the world around you to be, and in turn how self-disciplined you are. There is a good deal of scientific evidence supporting the benefits of a positive approach as it relates to motivation and discipline—not to mention benefits in other areas of life.

This chapter will dive into some of the ways to take on a more positive and optimistic outlook and the improvements that you'll see as a result.

The Endowed Progress Effect

One way to create a more disciplined mindset is to use what's known as the *endowed progress effect,* which states that you should think in terms of what you already have. For example, a video game where you earn coins or points as you play might give you a bunch of coins or points to begin with so that you are more likely to get engaged with the game.

The general idea is that people will work harder to achieve something if they are aware of all the ways that they are not starting from zero and closer to completion. So if you provide some sort of artificial progress toward a goal, that would then increase the probability of a person putting in the rest of the work to complete the goal.

Researchers Joseph C. Nunes and Xavier Dreze tested this theory in a clever way using loyalty cards for a car washing company. They handed out two different cards—one requiring eight purchases to earn a free car wash and the other requiring 10 but having two spaces already stamped. Regardless of which card a customer received, they all required an equal amount of effort to earn a free car wash. Yet the artificial advancement toward the goal created with the cards that already had two stamps led to a significant result. Nine months after giving out the cards, 34% of the people who were given cards with two free stamps had gone on to redeem them, while only 19% of those who were given the cards without free stamps had.

The endowed progress effect works by reducing the perceived amount of effort that's necessary to accomplish a goal while increasing the feeling of progress already made toward it. As a result, people will be more likely to then make the effort to reach the goal. This concept of endowed—or awarded—progress is different and affects motivation differently than earned progress. A customer who has gotten three car washes and needs to get seven more to earn a free one might feel differently than a customer who has the same three stamps but was awarded two of them for free.

While these examples describe scenarios where advertising can use the endowed progress effect in a somewhat manipulative way, the lesson from it is still valuable if applied to your daily self-discipline practices.

If you can think of ways that you have already made progress toward a goal or are starting with a leg up, you can make it more likely that you'll maintain discipline in pursuit of that goal. You should quantify your progress visually and figuratively so that you feel that you are far away from a starting point at zero. If you've already invested in achieving a goal in some way, you can contemplate how it would feel to waste whatever time, effort, and resources you've invested if you don't follow through and accomplish the goal.

Think about how you can quantify the progress you've already made, even if you haven't actually started yet. You have certain traits, capacities, and advantages that put you farther along than many others. They count!

For example, say your goal is to learn to play the guitar. You may have never played a real guitar in your life, but that doesn't mean you haven't made some progress. Maybe you already have good finger dexterity from playing another instrument or playing Guitar Hero. Perhaps you already learned how to read music, or know somebody who can give you lessons. You might even have a friend who will lend you their guitar so that you don't have to save up money to buy one. You may have played ukulele when you were younger for a few months. All of those things will make the time and effort necessary for you to learn the guitar less than if you were starting from zero, and that can motivate you to do it. You're starting from 20% instead of 0% and this can feel significant.

Goal Proximity

A similar concept to the endowed progress effect is the idea of *goal proximity*, which states that the closer we get to a goal, the more effort we make to reach it.

The hypothesis was first developed in the 1930s by research psychologist Clark Hall, who observed during an experiment that rats who were running a maze ran faster the closer they got to food. There was another researcher in the following decade, Judson Brown, who took a modified approach to the study. He attached harnesses to rats that were running toward food and then measured how strongly they pulled the harness as their distance from the food varied. Similar to Hall and his maze experiment, Brown found that the rats exerted more effort the closer they were to the food.

In this case, our brains don't work all that differently from those of rats. Feeling like we haven't made any progress toward a goal can make that goal seem unachievable or perhaps simply not worthwhile. But again, injecting any kind of artificial progress toward the goal can provide actual momentum to help you accomplish it because it will feel closer.

One example that illustrates goal proximity beautifully is the case of marathon runners, who run the 26th mile faster than most of the miles that preceded it. Theoretically, runners should be the slowest and the most tired at the very end of the marathon. Yet they consistently run that last portion faster, because they know they've almost reached their goal. If you can see the finish line—literally or figuratively—you're more likely to make the final push to reach it.

This principle, combined with the previous one, means you should always keep track of your progress and make sure to note each accomplishment, no matter how small. Emphasize how far away from starting from 0% you are, and how close to 100% you are.

Think of How Your Actions Can Benefit Others

Most people feel happy when they can bring positivity and benefits to other people's lives. Considering how your actions will impact those around you can be a powerful source of motivation to be disciplined and do what's right.

A psychological scientist at the University of Pennsylvania's Wharton School, Adam Grant, found in his research that thinking about how our actions can affect others is sometimes an even stronger motivator than anything personal. Grant learned that hospitals typically try to persuade medical staff to be diligent about handwashing by warning them that failing to wash their hands frequently after seeing patients increases the likelihood of getting sick. As it turns out, however, that isn't the most effective type of warning.

While healthcare professionals generally know that washing their hands consistently is important, they still only wash their hands about a third to a half of the time that they are exposed to patients with germs or contagious diseases. This can be attributed to what psychologists call "the illusion of invulnerability"—an explanation for why people irrationally believe that they aren't at risk of getting sick.

Moreover, Grant realized that signs warning doctors and nurses to wash their hands for the sake of their own health were ineffective, so he designed an experiment in which two signs were tested against each other—one saying "hand hygiene prevents you from catching diseases" and the other saying "hand hygiene prevents patients from catching diseases." The signs were placed in different locations around the hospital, which were then monitored to see how often doctors and nurses washed their hands—even going so far as to measure how much soap and sanitizing gel was used.

The sign advocating for handwashing in order to protect patients resulted in 10% more frequent handwashing and 33% more soap and sanitizing gel use per dispenser relative to the sign warning about personal risks.

So apart from the insight about the minds of medical professionals, what can we learn from Grant's research?

We should think about how our actions affect others front and center. This caring can either act as a powerful motivator, or it can work as a tool for shaming us into better behavior. We've talked in earlier chapters about how the relationships you keep have a marked effect on your discipline and life. This is just another way the people around you can influence your behavior.

For instance, we've talked about fitness as an example of building self-discipline, and how the concept of a workout partner will help your accountability. But why exactly does the workout partner help? Because you don't want to let them down. According to Grant's work, you can also be motivated by thinking about how you are helping your partner's life and fitness levels. In moments when you are feeling tired, being accountable to yourself typically isn't enough, and so thinking about the way that your sloth can negatively impact others will be more effective. On the other hand, thinking about how you can motivate and inspire somebody else to exercise by putting forth your best effort can give you the extra bit of perseverance you need to stay on track.

Think Optimistically

An ideal approach to life that is conducive to self-discipline can be summed up as being realistically optimistic—hoping for the best while preparing for the worst.

Try to consistently take a glass half-full view and look for the positives in everything that happens. That will be conducive to self-discipline because having a positive mindset prepares you to manage failure and discouragement—inevitable parts of genuine personal growth. Rather than dwelling on those setbacks, you'll learn from them and move on. You won't be discouraged because you expected setbacks, but you'll feel that the best is yet to come.

Being optimistic is a process of self-persuasion.

In other words, you *choose* to see the world in a positive light and to let go of your addiction to negativity and drama. Of course, becoming optimistic will take lots of time and effort. It would be great if you could just say, "I'm going to be optimistic from now on"—and for it to actually happen. As that isn't the case, though, the path of least resistance for becoming optimistic is one focused on daily awareness and self-discipline in both thoughts and actions.

As you gradually develop a more optimistic approach, you'll find it easier and easier to avoid people and situations that are negative or unproductive. You'll also see hope and potential where before you saw nothing. Instead of being bogged down by problems, you'll be full of solutions and a willingness to try them.

Perhaps the most important thing that happens when you focus on being optimistic is that you begin to attract other positive thinkers who can influence you to do bigger and better things for yourself. And instead of wasting time that you can never get back, you pursue activities and work that feeds and nourishes you on all levels.

So how will that optimism help you to be disciplined?

Imagine that you've just experienced a difficult breakup that left you brokenhearted and lonely. A pessimist might get caught up thinking that they'll never find the same amount of love and happiness with another partner, or dwell on regrets and mistakes made during the relationship. They'll be emotionally scarred for months and distrusting of humans in general. An optimist, on the other hand, will take it as an opportunity for personal growth, examine their role, and then seek love again with an open heart. While the pessimist takes months or even years to move on, the optimist will be equipped to process and learn from the breakup while still being productive and enjoying their life.

We all experience tough times; it's an optimistic attitude that helps some people remain disciplined and productive in those times while others lose sight of their dreams and goals.

Think in Terms of Effort

A lot of things that happen to us and around us are out of our control. When we focus on what we can control—our own effort—our mindset becomes much healthier. Outcomes, despite how much effort we might put toward them, are 100% up to external influences.

As long as you focus on outcomes and attach self-worth to them, you'll be closed off to new experiences and taking risks. In fact, if you are worried about failing, you might even try less in the first place so that you don't have to face the prospect of giving it your all and it not being enough. On the other hand, when you only attach your sense of worth to the effort you're putting forth, you start to enjoy the process regardless of the outcome.

That doesn't mean that you won't still have goals, but rather you should subtly switch your goals. Instead of shooting for the outcome itself, which is impossible to control, your goal should be to put in your best effort at the present moment. You can control that and feel good about it.

Whenever you feel trapped or just stuck where you are in life, ask yourself whether you're focusing on outcomes and what people think of you, or if you are engaged in the process of pursuing your goals and truly living in the present. When you are enjoying the journey, you can fully express and manifest your gifts and talents in a way that often leads to more positive outcomes.

Flawed efforts can still lead to success and perfect efforts can still result in failure. Therefore, it's important to detach your performance from outcomes because that will prevent you from reinforcing the wrong techniques. You'll be able to learn and develop new skills more efficiently if you're able to realize the things that you did well in your process regardless of whether or not it leads to the desired outcome in each particular case.

For example, say that you have a goal to learn to speak basic Italian in three months before taking a trip to Italy. It would be a great practice of discipline if you can study every day consistently for 15 minutes per day, even though that isn't much time. You might arrive in Italy and be disappointed to realize that you don't understand native speakers who talk really fast. But that doesn't detract at all from the fact that you consistently made an effort to learn and that you can at least speak a lot more Italian than the typical tourist.

This all comes down to focusing on what you can control. Most of the time, you'll only have partial control over final outcomes in your life but you can completely control the process that you use. You are fully capable of giving your best effort every single time.

Takeaway: There are a few ways to approach life, work, and obstacles to make sure you stay on the self-disciplined path. If you feel that you have already made progress in some way, you are more likely to continue (the endowed progress effect). If you feel that you are relatively close to the finishing point, you are more likely to continue (goal proximity). If you actively think about how you are helping others instead of just yourself, you are more likely to continue. Finally, if you are more optimistic, you will definitely be more likely to continue.

Chapter 11. Build Routines and Habits for Ultimate Self-Discipline

When it comes to self-discipline and reaching your goals, do you think having the habit of discipline or sufficient motivation is more important?

You might be thinking that it's motivation because delaying gratification and accepting temporary discomfort is difficult to do without being highly motivated. In reality, creating and developing good habits of self-discipline is exponentially more important than motivation in terms of reaching goals and getting what you want. And the reason is simple—motivation is temporary, no matter how much of it you have. It is a reaction, an emotion, and these things dry up. Habits, on the other hand, are consistent and they are necessary to make self-discipline sustainable.

Motivation Doesn't Last

It's much sexier and flashier to motivate people rather than talk to them about the benefits of good habits. But motivation is a temporary state of mind, while habits become ingrained behaviors. Which sounds more sustainable: a pep talk to dig holes for 12 hours, or the habit of digging holes as a matter of fact?

Motivation is an emotional response consisting of excitement, desire, and willingness to take action—all positive emotions that one feels in anticipation of pursuing a goal. Motivation is important; I even had a chapter about motivation in this book. Sometimes, the most powerfully we act can be tied to powerful motivation. The problem with motivation is that it is fleeting, and will usually fade away after hours or even days—weeks in the best of scenarios.

Discipline requires the repetitive action of habits because when people lose their motivation and emotional attachment, they see all of that disciplined action for what it is—uncomfortable work.

Losing motivation doesn't mean that you lose your desire to accomplish something. After several weeks have passed and your motivation is fading, you'll still want to get into medical school, start your own business, or overcome an addiction. But what happens when, inevitably, "wanting" something isn't enough to put in the effort necessary to get it? More than likely, you have a lapse in discipline or stop pursuing your goal entirely.

Mostly through the passage of time and repetition, we eventually lose our emotional attachment to all motivated behavior. The euphoric feelings associated with the motivation will fade away. Unlike fleeting emotional states, the habit of discipline is a rational thought process that becomes a permanent way of living once it's developed.

The addict who wants to finally overcome their addiction will only be successful if he or she diligently attends support group meetings, goes to therapy sessions, and takes the prescribed medication on schedule. Motivation is wanting to beat the addiction. Discipline is doing all of those things to make it a reality.

Forming Habits Takes Time

In the words of Aristotle, "Good habits formed at youth make all the difference." Building habits is thought to be easier in youth because our minds are more malleable, but altering habits is possible regardless of age.

Phillippa Lally, a health psychology researcher at University College London, published a study in the *European Journal of Social Psychology* that aimed to find out just how long the process of habit formation really takes. The study was conducted over the course of 12 weeks and examined the behavior of 96 participants who chose habits that they would try to build and then reported daily on how automatic the behavior felt. After analyzing the data, Lally and her team determined that, on average, it took 66 days for a daily action to become automatic.

How long it takes you to develop a new habit will depend on your existing habits and behavior as well as your personal circumstances. The quickest habit in Lally's study was developed in only 18 days, while the slowest took 254 days.

Positive habits are crucial to self-discipline because once you have a habit, it's second nature. You can think of good habits like frozen, automatic self-discipline that guides you to where you want to go in life. They are your subconscious, automatic response that doesn't require extra effort on your part.

Something that initially requires a lot of self-discipline, for example, is daily exercise. So to build that habit, you might schedule it at the same time every day and then give yourself a little reward immediately afterward to incentivize yourself to do it. After a month (or two months, as Lally's study found), you won't even need much self-discipline anymore, so long as you stick to your habits.

The lesson here is straightforward. Building habits takes time, and it requires self-discipline to get through that process. But once you make it through that phase, your habit will drive you to achieve where you used to require exercising self-discipline. Expect that you will require at least two months.

It will take quite a while for the annoyance and discomfort of forming self-discipline habits to vanish. You might still feel them on rare occasions, but having already built the habit will make it much easier to control whatever negative urges do arise.

First, avoid self-sabotage. That means that you want to start small and manageable with habits rather than shooting for the stars right away and guaranteeing failure. If you're out of shape and want to get fit, start with taking a 20-

minute walk every day rather than immediately jumping into a workout routine that will make you sore and miserable. Twenty minutes of walking is such an attainable goal that it's impossible to come up with an excuse not to do it.

Starting small reduces the perceived difficulty of the task and will make it easier to stick with it when your motivation is lacking. It tells your brain that this action is acceptable and even enjoyable. It also builds a level of anticipation and expectation for the action. And of course, you can steadily increase the duration or difficulty of your new habit as you feel yourself progressing.

Whenever you do feel highly motivated in the initial stages of habit formation, you can certainly take advantage of that to make bigger strides toward your goal. But keep in mind that being disciplined and putting in the effort will not always feel exhilarating. And if you can't do it when it feels bad or you feel annoyed, the habit isn't going to stick. So savor the motivation when you have it, but don't get addicted to that feeling.

Some days will be easy and you'll use positive emotions to overachieve. There will also be plenty of times when emotion runs low and you really have to tap into your willpower and self-discipline to fulfill the habit formation process. But if you persevere for long enough, the rollercoaster ride eventually comes to a halt and your new behavior becomes a habit and a permanent part of your life. Tasks that once required mental fortitude will become as easy and natural as breathing.

Don't Wait for It to "Feel Right"

It turns out there is a very logical explanation for why forming new habits and breaking old ones is so difficult.

Charles Duhigg, author of *The Power of Habit*, explains that habit behaviors correlate with high activity in a part of the brain called the basal ganglia—a region of the brain that's associated with emotions, patterns, and memories. The basal ganglia is completely separate from the prefrontal cortex where—as you likely know—we make our decisions. That means that when behaviors become habits, we stop using our decision-making skills and instead function on auto-pilot.

What is the primary takeaway from that information? When you try to break a bad habit or form a positive one, you're naturally going to feel awkward or uncomfortable at first because you have to actively make decisions about your behavior. Your brain has already been programmed to function in a certain way, so it will resist the change and, as a result, make the new behavior feel wrong and even frightening.

The best thing to do in order to successfully reprogram your behavior is to embrace the wrong. Your new routine is going to take a while to start feeling right or natural, so just accept that and keep chugging along. Eventually, the behavior you want will be wired into your basal ganglia and you can go back to auto-pilot as an improved version of yourself.

Habit formation will start with feelings of unease rather than feelings of excitement and comfort.

Ultimately, habit formation and self-discipline come down to small actions persisting over 66 days that you must power through without regard to your emotional state. What are some ways you can start forming habits for self-discipline in 66 days or less?

Furthermore, think about how you can turn small actions into solid habits by slowly escalating them. For instance, you could start a habit of exercising by first jogging for one lap around the block, and gradually increasing every week. One block turns into two blocks, and then three, and so on. Try to build all of your habits in this way, where you constantly push yourself to reach slightly higher, but attainable goals.

Few things that are worthwhile in life come easily—discipline is no different. But you want to break bad habits and form positive ones for a reason. Acknowledge that it's going to take a lot of hard work, and then just get started.

The Six Sources of Influence Model

Joseph Grenny and his team of collaborators developed a model that can help you change your behavior and succeed in the process of habit formation—the Six Sources of Influence Model. The model explains all of the factors that influence us whenever we try to alter our behavior or increase our discipline. These are all of the obstacles you face in forming habits and even just acting in a disciplined manner.

Here's the breakdown of influences along with examples of how they might impact somebody who is trying to make a behavior change, such as quitting smoking:

- Individual
    - Personal motivation—are you motivated to quit smoking to improve your health and lifestyle? What's in it for you and how does your life improve?
    - Personal ability—are you personally capable of overcoming the physical and

mental addictiveness of smoking? Do you have enough willpower or social support? Is there a family history of addiction?

- Society
  - Social motivation—do you have friends and family who will encourage you to quit and avoid offering you cigarettes or smoking around you? Are you facing social pressure to continue or quit smoking?
  - Social ability—do you know anybody who's successfully quit before or do you have access to support groups? Are your friends all heavy smokers?
- Environment
  - Structural motivation—does your everyday living environment punish you for smoking, such as with fines for smoking indoors?
  - Structural ability—do you have reminders built into your everyday living environment and context to encourage quitting smoking?

Let's take an even deeper look. The first category of influence is the individual—you—

and is based on your personal motivation and ability. Personal motivation is a simple matter of how badly you want to do something, while personal ability refers to whether or not you are capable of doing it.

Motivation is fleeting but you still need it to succeed, and so you can get more motivation by making your actions as fun and enjoyable as possible while also making sure that you've chosen a goal that's aligned with your values. At the same time, new habits are often much more intellectually, physically, and emotionally challenging than they first seem.

Say, for example, you want to get into the best shape of your life. You should ask yourself if that desire to be more fit is motivated by a desire to be better at some athletics, or a wish to improve confidence and self-esteem. Do you know how to exercise safely and effectively? What about healthy nutrition? Ideally, you can give honest responses to those type of questions that indicate that your goal is realistic.

If so, the next category of influence you could consider is society—the people around you. As with individual influence, societal influence is part motivation and part ability. Social motivation refers to how positively or negatively the people around you influence your behavior, and social ability refers to how much help you'll have to maintain positive behavior until it becomes habitual.

Ideally, your friends and family will support you by encouraging healthy behavior and discouraging negative behavior. Better yet, they can contribute to your success by providing necessary help, information, and resources to aid you in the process of learning a new habit or skill.

So in your quest to get into the best shape of your life, you would ask yourself if the people around you give you positive reinforcement when you're doing well and hold you accountable when you skip workouts or eat unhealthy food. Do you have a personal trainer or coach to help you with your exercise regimen, and is your family eating a healthy diet with you or at least keeping unhealthy food out of the areas where it could tempt you?

Then, finally, there's the environment—all of the nonhuman factors surrounding you on a daily basis. Environmental influence can be referred to as "structure" and is also broken down into motivation and ability. Structural motivation is simply how your environment encourages you to do the right behavior by rewarding you for doing well and inflicting some negative consequence when your discipline lapses. Structural ability, meanwhile, is whether or not your environment supports you with reminders and cues to keep you on track.

Have you set up a system to reward yourself for sticking to your diet and exercise regimen and to punish yourself when you don't maintain it? Maybe you can watch your favorite TV show while you ride the exercise bike at the gym but not allow yourself to watch it if you miss a workout out due to sloth. You can further influence yourself to reach your fitness goals by giving yourself cues to stay on course such as always working out at the same time and doing meal prep so that you'll have healthy food prepared when you don't feel like cooking.

It's so common to think about discipline as black and white—either you have the motivation and willpower or you don't. But motivation and willpower always fail you when you haven't optimized the other facets of your life for discipline. Anything can work in a vacuum, but very few methods can withstand scrutiny in the multi-faceted real world.

You need to accept that sometimes discipline is going to be difficult and it might feel extremely wrong, but that's temporary. If you push through the pain and discomfort that you'll inevitably face when you try to change your behavior, you can break bad habits and build better ones in their place. Choose attainable goals and then create a plan of action based on your personal motivation and ability as well as those of your social circles and environment.

But most importantly, just get started and don't stop putting in the effort until it discipline is as natural as breathing.

Takeaway: Motivation and self-discipline are nice to have. Motivation, however, is often emotional and temporary, while self-discipline can be exhausted. But having solid habits will deliver the same results with far less pain and suffering. Habits have been shown to take around 66 days to form, so all you need to do is commit to small actions (mini habits) for that amount of time. How successfully you are able to keep to your habits is in part influenced by Joseph Grenny's six factors of influence.

Summary Guide

Chapter 1. The Biological Basis of Self-Discipline

It may not be surprising that self-discipline has a biological basis. This means, like any of your muscles, it can be trained and also depleted and worn out. The latter is known as willpower fatigue. This is a good thing because it gives you a blueprint to deal with your self-discipline—you can increase it, and you can put yourself in situations to conserve it. It also means you can affect your self-discipline in positive ways through daily behaviors and habits.

Chapter 2. What Pushes Your Buttons?

Self-discipline is important, but so is having a proper motivation to make self-discipline unnecessary. What you think might motivate you may not in reality, so it's important to be honest with yourself. Studies have consistently shown material possessions to be a poor motivator. Instead, personal feelings of progress, autonomy, mastery, and purpose are far better motivators to attach yourself to. Other factors include extrinsic versus intrinsic motivators and Aristotle's theory of motivation.

Chapter 3. Discipline Tactics of Navy SEALs

Navy SEALs are routinely touted as masters of their willpower because it is the difference between life and death for them. They use a few tactics to keep taking action, the most well-known of which is the 40% Rule: when you think you've hit your limits, you're actually only at 40% capacity. Other tactics for discipline include box breathing for arousal control, setting big goals as a means to putting mind over matter, and the 10-Minute Rule.

Chapter 4. Diagnosing Discipline Drainers

A few common obstacles to discipline are setting your sights unrealistically high (False Hope Syndrome), procrastinating by striving for perfection (which can be combated by the 75% Rule), rationalizing excuses for inaction, and the effects of Parkinson's Law (which can be combated by setting aggressive deadlines).

Chapter 5. Flex Your "Uncomfortable Muscle"

Self-discipline is in itself an act of discomfort, so it makes sense to practice discomfort like a muscle. One of the most effective ways to practice discomfort is to "surf the urge" which has been shown to be better than actively resisting urges. Further, you can practice rejection therapy or simply put yourself in uncomfortable situations, mostly social, that will require you to act.

Chapter 6. Creating A Disciplined Environment

The environments you create for yourself has a huge impact on your self-discipline because it can either constantly drain it, or it can help you conserve and exercise it. You should strategically limit your distractions by employing "out of sight, out of mind," minimize dopamine spikes that sabotage your focus, and make the path of least resistance the action you want the most.

Chapter 7. The Relationships That Inform Our Willpower

More than our environments, we are perhaps most influenced by the relationships we keep. Our social circle informs us as to what is acceptable, can support us, or can hold us back. You can't choose your family, but you can choose whom you spend your time with, as well as proactively seek out mentors and role models to shore up your weaknesses.

Chapter 8. Why You Should Always Eat Your Vegetables First

The concept of delayed gratification is not new. It's the ability to eat your vegetables before you to eat your dessert. Studies have found that this simple ability is highly correlated with high performance in various aspects of life. Another way to look at it is to proactively think about your future self more—the one who will be rewarded for your temporary suffering. Finally, you can take a peek into the future with the 10-10-10 Rule: how will you feel or be affected 10 minutes, 10 hours, and 10 days after choosing a lapse in self-discipline?

Chapter 9. Quick! Read in Case of Temptation!

There are four broad and illuminating questions to immediately ask yourself in the face of any temptation, distraction, or impulse. Are you disciplined or not? Are you doing the easy thing or what's right? What are you getting for dessert? Are you being self-aware?

Chapter 10. Mindset and Approach Are Everything

There are a few ways to approach life, work, and obstacles to make sure you stay on the self-disciplined path. If you feel that you have already made progress in some way, you are more likely to continue (the endowed progress effect). If you feel that you are relatively close to the finishing point, you are more likely to continue (goal proximity). If you actively think about how you are helping others instead of just yourself, you are more likely to continue. Finally, if you are more optimistic, you will definitely be more likely to continue.

Chapter 11. Build Routines and Habits for Ultimate Self-Discipline

Motivation and self-discipline are nice to have. Motivation, however, is often emotional and temporary, while self-discipline can be exhausted. But having solid habits will deliver the same results with far less pain and suffering. Habits have been shown to take around 66 days to form, so all you need to do is commit to small actions (mini habits) for that amount of time. How successfully you are able to keep to your habits is in part influenced by Joseph Grenny's six factors of influence.

Lightning Source UK Ltd.
Milton Keynes UK
UKHW020040220920
370298UK00014B/735